Your Health and Information Technologies

George O. Obikoya

Table of Contents

Executive Summary

H ealthcare delivery is undergoing perhaps its most profound changes in history. From the health problems of an aging population that most developed countries grapple with, to pervasive unmet healthcare needs in much of the developing world, to the growing threat of an avian flu pandemic, the increasing focus on health is universal. Soaring healthcare costs perplex rich and poor countries alike. Health reforms seem inevitably to be in perpetual motion as nations desperately seek answers to runaway health spending, justifiably concerned at the alarming rate it is chipping at the core of their econom ies. The prevalence of preventable diseases is rising, the result, increasing ill health, lengthening hospitalizations, escalating medications costs, and increasing overall health spending. Payer-concern about these developments manifests in massive lay-offs, the public, flustered by the increasing difficulty accessing health services, even affording them in the first place. Colorectal or bowel cancer for example, is the second major cause of cancer-related deaths in Australia, second only to lung cancer, someone dying of the disease every two hours, yet up to 75% of bowel cancer is preventable through regular exercise and a healthy diet. These seemingly benign measures could also help reduce the risks of a number of other diseases such as diabetes, high blood pressure, and cardiovascular diseases, all of which are causes of significant morbidities that could result in chronic illnesses, even premature deaths. They are also some of the most important causes of rising healthcare costs in many countries. Given the facts that despite likely genetic predisposition to some of these diseases, they are largely preventable by relatively simple measures, yet their prevalence is increasing, in fact, to epidemic proportions in some cases, it is hardly surprising the demoralization of many by our seeming helplessness in solving crucial health problems. Recent developments in the health and related industries and among healthcare stakeholders appear to have ushered in a new era of health services delivery, and to signal the resolve of all concerned to end this evident downward drift of global health affairs. This e-book is about this promising new direction that healthcare heads. It focuses on the issues, problems, processes, obstacles, and solutions, and on the key underlying role that health information technologies play in all of these, and in the interplay of a variety of factors influencing events in the health industry that seem to be propelling it in this new direction. The book also conjectures on the outcomes of this intercourse and on their chances within the context of relentless technological progress, of generating new factors in a continuous paradigm shift in tandem with the changing face of health and related issues.

One of the changes occurring in the health industry is a shift in the power balance between health consumers and providers. Healthcare consumers are increasingly keen to participate in all matters relating to their health. They want to know more about health issues including staying healthy and about diseases that they or those they know have. The enormous amounts of health information on the Internet attest to this increasing thirst of the public for health information. The question, though, is whether this situation, what some consider an information glut, is serving the public well. Their skepticism predicates on the glaring inaccuracies, redundancies, and in some cases, outright biases, evident in the information. There is no doubt about the need to correct the information asymmetry prevalent in the health industry. The days of "paternalistic Medicine" should indeed, be over. Nonetheless, we do not want to replace it with something even worse, with the public fed with information that could prove detrimental, even dangerous to health. This is why it is important not only to have information technologies that could deliver, analyzed and targeted, current and timely health information to those that need them, but also some means of regulating health information flow on the World Wide Web (WWW). Furthermore, this targeted information delivery constitutes an integral and indeed, indispensable aspect of the new consumer-driven healthcare paradigm, which seems to be gaining increasing currency in many developed countries. The basic idea behind this healthcare delivery model is for patients to have the option of choosing their healthcare providers. Since they would have to pay for some of their healthcare costs, the model assumes that they would be more discerning in making those choices. This assumption is fine except that one could only make rational choices armed with vital information that would help in that exercise, which underscores the need for accurate and current targeted information delivery. How would a senior for example know to request his/her doctor to prescribe a generic rather a brand medication not even knowing generics exist? How much in medication costs could such a senior have saved knowing about the alternative generics that the doctor could prescribe? Some individuals with Diabetes who check their blood sugars on their own may not discard some manufacturers' strips after the third month that they opened the bottle s cap, the strips expiry date, regardless. May be they do not because they do not know that they should, although the instruction is actually on the outside of the bottle. Now, if some people did not read the instructions outside the bottle containing the medications they used, there would be some, perhaps even more, that do not read the information leaflet inside the bottle. Some would argue that it is a shame that people do not do that. Fair enough but should we give up on them because of that, and in particularly did the manufacturers not have some reason for that instruction? Considering that, the reason could be that the strips do not work reliably after three months of exposure, could some people be taking comfort in false blood sugar readings or needlessly alarmed? Could someone be taking additional insulin when the blood sugar is actually dipping or not taking it when diabetic ketoacidosis is imminent? What are the implications of these false readings for the burden of diabetes on families and society on the aggregate, including on already escalating health spending? Should we not be doing something about letting everyone with diabetes know about this warning? Could the deployment of appropriate information technologies not help in this regard? Is there not a need for collaborative efforts among healthcare stakeholders for example, the family doctor, the pharmacist, drug manufacturing firms, and health plans in ensuring that patients receive targeted health information? This example illustrates how different factors interweave to create a health problem and the issues surrounding it, and how health information technologies underlie these issues and the solutions to them. Additionally, it shows the need for urgent considerations of policy changes as this interplay of factors and information technologies often have important implications for disease prevention and treatment, and of course the outcomes of illnesses and healthcare costs. We will explore these issues in this book including the technologies emerging for dealing with them, for example the collaboration between the health industry and Semantic Web experts to improve the applications of Semantic Web technologies, the next generation of the WWW technologies relying substantially on ontologies and metadata, to healthcare delivery.

The book also explores the applications of health information technologies to health with particular respect to women, children, men, and other groups. Falls for example are common in the elderly and could result in life threatening consequences. New information technologies could help these falls. Slips, unsteady gait, poor balance control, and strokes cause up to 60 per cent of falls in people regardless of age, although risk factors such frailty, home trip hazards, medications, and visual impairment, also play a part. There are now wearable portable devices that measure body movement, store and analyze these measurements, and help prevent falls, and some even raise an alarm and transmit it to a helper. Electronic health records (EHR), computerized physician order entry (CPOE), radiofrequency identification (RFID), and bar codes, are other healthcare technologies that have the potential to improve healthcare delivery, and reduce healthcare costs. However, their reception by healthcare providers is still slow. This book examines the issues hindering healthcare ICT diffusion, such as information privacy and confidentiality, and those critical to expediting ICT adoption, for example new technologies' development such as Commonwealth Scientific and Industrial Research Organization(CSIRO)'s new Privacy-Preserving Analytics (PPA) algorithms. The PPA, incorporated on CSIRO's prototype, Privacy-Preserving Linking (PPL) technology, which encrypts any data that identifies patients but also enables the analysis of all non-identifiable data, facilitates data and information communication and sharing without breaching privacy. Information transmission is at the core of the benefits of health information technologies, the existing and emerging technologies that facilitate the achievement of which objective this book also explores in detail.

Introduction

"Cancer chemical found in drinks," screamed the headlines of a BBC news item on March 01, 2006. The news organization reported findings of traces of a cancer-causing chemical in British soft drinks at eight times the level permitted in drinking water. Although the UK Food Standards Agency (FSA) reassured the public that these levels do not pose an immediate health risk, questions linger on answers to which many would be eager to have. The chemical, benzene, known to cause certain cancers, forms when two commonly used ingredients in soft drinks react, the results announced obtained from industry tests prompted by the FSA after tests on drinks in the US revealed the presence of the chemical. The BBC passed the American results to the FSA, which then requested firms to carry out the tests. The industry tests on 230 different products revealed levels of up to eight parts per billion in some soft drinks, the brand names of these drinks yet unrevealed. There is a legal limit of one part per billion on the amount of benzene permissible in drinking water, but there are no UK restrictions on the amount of the chemical allowed in soft drinks. The soft drinks industry has known for over a decade that the preservative sodium benzoate can produce benzene if mixed with ascorbic acid, also known as Vitamin C, raising questions regarding why they are still present in many soft drinks. Furthermore, there appears to be an association between benzene, also a component of vehicle exhaust fumes, and leukemia and other blood cancers. FSA is asking the public not to panic and to await the outcome of further investigations, promising to act accordingly to protect the consumer if necessary. To further reassure the public experts claim that an urban city dweller consumes, on average, 400 micrograms of benzene from exhaust fumes per day, equivalent to consuming 40 liters of a soft drink containing benzene at just over the World Health Organization guideline level of 10 parts per billion. Some consumer advocates however, remain unimpressed, insisting that producers put vitamin C in soft drinks to make them more attractive to buy as health drinks, as most market them to children in particular, emphasizing the need for parents and consumers to know the constituents of these drinks. In fact, some even argue that scientific evidence is ambiguous about whether there is any safe level of benzene. Should consumers indeed not have relevant and current information on the carcinogenicity or otherwise of benzene, its safety in soft drinks, for children and other consumers, and why ascorbic acid is back in soft drinks, among other pertinent information on this issue? This example illustrates the increasing importance of health information to the consumer in the current dispensation of healthcare delivery, one increasingly concerned about and seeking ways to ensure patient safety.

T he US Institute of Medicine IOM) released its famed "To err is human" report

in 2000 alerting us all to the high mortality resulting from medical errors in the US healthcare system, thousands of Americans dying yearly. There have since been calls by the public, government, private organizations, interest groups, and others for healthcare providers to institute safety measures to prevent these needless deaths. Many have specifically recommended the use of ICT such as CPOE, bar codes, and e-prescribing by healthcare providers in order to safe lives. Nonetheless, progress in healthcare ICT diffusion has been slow for very many reasons ranging from costs, to security, privacy, and confidentiality issues, and to technical issues such as integration with legacy systems. Meanwhile people are still dying in hospitals due to medical errors according to a recent study published in the Journal of the American Medical Association released on May 19, 2005. The report showed that as many as 98,000 Americans still die annually due to medical errors, five years after the first IOM report. Some of the factors the researchers at the Harvard's School of Public Health attributed this problem to include the complexity of health care systems, a lack of leadership, the reluctance of doctors to admit errors and an insurance reimbursement system that rewards errors. In particular the researchers noted that health insurers reimburse hospitals for additional services required for injured patients, but usually do not reimburse practices that reduce errors. The researchers also noted the significance of computerized prescriptions, among other information technologies, in improving patient safety. These efforts along with those of various bodies advocating patient safety have resulted in up to 93% reductions in certain types of illnesses and deaths due to medical errors. Dr Leape, co-author of the study suggested that rather than keep paying for health services as is currently the case, payment should rather be for care and outcomes, for example, insurers reimbursing hospitals that eliminate infections. This study has brought the issue of patient safety, and the role healthcare ICT could play in eliminating medical errors and saving lives squarely to the fore. Yet, despite its promise, the large-scale deployment of health information technologies appears painfully slow. This is mainly due to the skepticism of the people that will use the technologies, that is, the clinicians, as there is increasing evidence that the public is increasingly favorably disposed toward healthcare ICT. Clinicians and hospital administrators just do not seem to trust the IT industry to deliver safe ICT, not to mention other issues such as costs, and the technophobia, that some doctors would unlikely deny that they have. This has made it almost impossible for the industry to get independent medical practitioners and small physician groups in particular to embrace electronic medical records (EMR,) critical to the communication and sharing of patient information that assuring patient safety demands. Without the participation of small medical practices, we can say goodbye to the concept of a healthcare network, some contend, despite the spirited efforts of the Canadian, American and other governments in the developed world to encourage its widespread deployment. Should we blame doctors for the problem? In the past, technology solutions were indeed, too costly for sole practitioners and small group practices. The solutions were also very unreliable, for a variety of reasons, some technical, others, software development management-related. This combination essentially priced the very people expected to use the technology out of the market, which prompted some to suggest that perhaps software and ICT companies need to rethink its pricing and other policies for EMRs and other health information technologies. On the other hand, there are also suggestions that governments should continue to pursue their goals of making the use electronic medical records standard practice, and should continue to support efforts by the private sector to develop certification standards for ambulatory EMRs, among other efforts to encourage the more pervasive use of healthcare ICT in the healthcare delivery. Vendors are for sure making efforts to cut down prices and set industry-wide standards and should continue to do so. Indeed, the more widespread the use of healthcare information technologies, the likelier their prices would fall due to the operations of market forces. Doctors should recognize the potential value of EMRs and other healthcare ICT to high-quality healthcare delivery and not see ICT as having a negative business value. One way to avoid ICT having a negative impact on their practices finances, for example, is for doctors to engage in the strategic planning of ICT investments to meet the mission that they set out to achieve for their practices. There is no doubt that patient safety is non-negotiable, and the widespread adoption of healthcare information technologies, which would likely assure this goal, requires the concerted efforts of all healthcare stakeholders.

E-prescribing software provides an important opportunity for healthcare providers to ensure patient safety, and collaborative efforts are ongoing among a variety of stakeholders to promote the increasing use of e-prescribing in healthcare delivery. On October 29, 2004, Allscripts Healthcare Solutions (Nasdaq: MDRX) announced a joint effort with Cisco Systems to give a 30-day free trial version CD of TouchScript.NETTM at the National Conference on m-Health and EOE, and via the TouchScript website. The two firms recognize the crucial impact of assisting physicians to evolve their practices to mobile health and electronic order entry processes and move away from the highly inefficient, paper-based, manual prescription processes fraught with errors and that compromise patient safety. The TouchScript.NET solution is accessible via the Internet with industry-leading security features, and makes it possible for physicians to swiftly prescribe, check for drug interactions, access medication histories, review drug reference information, and send prescriptions straight to the pharmacy. The firms are hoping that the free trial of the e-prescribing software will encourage physicians to evaluate e-prescribing and understand the value of this technology without financial risk, removing a significant barrier to adoption. A practice only needs a PC to use TouchScript.NET. For interested practices, TouchScript.NET also works with hand-held connectivity into a wireless network. Practices that decide to keep writing prescriptions electronically can purchase the system at a low subscription cost. Designed as the first module of a complete electronic medical record, TouchScript helps doctors to boost patient safety, reduce pharmacy callbacks, and improve office efficiency. The expectation is that the software will meet the real need for a cost-effective system for smaller practices who are concerned with the cost of automating their traditional paper systems. In a February 13, 2006, press release, the company announced its selection for Health and Human Services (HHS) e-prescribing pilot, its clients to participate in two eRx pilots, testing standards and interoperability. The firm will collaborate with two research teams studying electronic prescribing standards through pilot tests that the U.S. Department of Health & Human Services (HHS) is funding. Administered jointly by the Centers for Medicare & Medicaid Services (CMS) and the Agency for Healthcare Research and Quality (AHRQ), the project is set to go. Already allocated $6 million to fund cooperative agreements to test initial standards for e-prescribing in part with the Medicare Modernization Act (MMA), which encourages health plans to support physicians' use of e-prescribing and adoption of standards to promote interoperability, the project is truly intersectoral. It involves at different stages the participation of research organizations, for example, the RAND Corporation, and universities, such as Brown and Midwestern, Health Plans, for example, Horizon Blue Cross Blue Shield of New Jersey, the electronic prescription routing firms RxHub and SureScripts, and pharmacies, such as Walgreen's retail pharmacies, among others. The project will evaluate a number of standards including medication history, standards for formulary and benefit information received from payers and the use of standardized formats for patient instructions and drug vocabularies. The pilot will also evaluate how the standards work in a variety of practice settings and geographic locations and how prescriber features affect the technology's adoption. The HHS e-prescribing pilot will last one year, and will no doubt improve knowledge of this valuable technology and reveal areas of improvements in both technology and practice that would further help promote its use among doctors and reassure patients that it would indeed, ensure their safety.

Mobile technology is also making medical practice safer for patients.

Clinicians can now conveniently access vital prescription drug information on the fly via the latest mobile technology. Physicians, nurses, and other healthcare professionals can access a variety of current drug and laboratory information at the point of care, thereby reducing the chances of medical errors. Clinicians and nurses can access information on dosing, side effects, precautions, drug interactions, and other important information on more than 3,500 drugs and herbals. They can instantly view information on over a thousand disorders and hundreds of diagnostic tests and panels. There is even a doc alert messaging system, which delivers brief medical news alerts to the doctor's mobile device, and gives him/her the option of requesting more information. Epocrates is one such software behind this functionality of mobile technologies. It is a hand-held drug reference application designed for the Palm OS and Pocket PC platforms. Epocrates Rx Online(TM) reference is available for Internet-connected desktop computers. The doctor could download it readily, and related products via the Internet and Epocrates Essentials is free. There are also Epocrates Rx(R) and Epocrates Rx Pro(TM) drug reference products. The doctor could use this versatile drug reference to check formulary status, prior authorization requirements, alternatives, generic substitutes, and quantity limits. It is useful to calculate drug doses, check for contra indications to their use, their adverse reactions, how much they cost, and with Epocrates MultiCheck(R) function, to check up to 30 drugs simultaneously for interactions. Epocrates makes it possible for clinicians to identify promptly the most appropriate drug to give a patient, hence improving the quality of their care. Physicians are also able to access cost information and integrate this crucial factor into their discussions with their patients, which is quite important for health insurance purposes. Consider the benefits that someone who had to cut down on drugs because he or she could not afford it would derive from now being able to discuss such issues frankly with the doctor, who in turn is now able to ask if the patient can afford the drugs, and suggest affordable alternatives. Because they are able to access drug-reference information, co-pay schedules, health plan formularies, availability of lower cost generics, and even an estimate of drugs retail prices at the point-of-care (POC), health care professionals using Epocrates can now discuss essentially all aspects of treatment with their patients. Efforts to developed healthcare ICT that would further assure patient safety and improve the quality of healthcare delivery continue. Intel, renowned for its ubiquitous Pentium processor technology, announced on February 27, 2006 at a briefing in San Francisco that it has begun to develop prototypes of specialized computers that could help medical professionals, as well as patients in the domiciliary management of chronic health problems, according to the *Wall Street Journal.* For medical professionals, tablet computers could automatically locate the correct medical records when doctors approach patients with an ID tag that transmits a radio signal, according to company officials. Further, the computers could include a high-tech stethoscope and camera to share information with healthcare professionals in disparate areas, and for the home, could include touch screens, which could display vital information, to help patients with Alzheimer's disease and other health conditions. Intel plans to start large-scale tests of some of the computers and related software in 2006, and to help develop standards for computer systems to allow hospitals and health clinics to share information. The company although conceded that an agreement on standards for the diverse computer systems used by autonomous physicians, labs, hospitals and health insurers will take years and require intersectoral collaboration, including with the health industry and federal government. There is no doubt about the need for such collaboration in other areas of healthcare in order to improve health services delivery.

The quest for such collaborative efforts to broaden support and strengthen

their respective administrative simplification efforts was behind the formation of a coalition, the Healthcare Administrative Simplification Coalition (HASC), recently of a range of stakeholders including physicians, hospitals, health plans, employers, labor, and government. The coalition aims to identify strategies for reducing the costs and administrative complexity of the US healthcare system. Since its inception, HASC has assembled three times in Washington, DC, and endorsed the successful work of the Council for Affordable Quality Healthcare in two of the coalition s key areas of interest. These areas are to help reduce redundancy in the process of credentialing physicians and other healthcare professionals to permit them to participate in health plans and to provide services in hospitals and other organizations; and to standardize processes for identifying and confirming patient insurance coverage, including co-payment or deductible amounts. The coalition will also be establishing a communications campaign to expand awareness of the price of administrative complexity and redundancy, important objectives that would facilitate overall efforts at improving healthcare delivery, and which one cannot minimize the key input of health information technologies in achieving. The US Agency for Healthcare Research and Quality (AH RQ) recently announced three public meetings in March 2006, to understand the "thinking and plans of providers that are interested in seeking out patient safety organization (PSO) services, and of entities that anticipate establishing such an organization". This is another clear evidence of the significance that various stakeholders ascribe to patient safety, and to collaborative efforts to achieve it. At the core of the value of health information technologies, including improving patient safety is the ability to communicate and share patient information among disparate healthcare providers and other healthcare stakeholders. This is why electronic health records (EHR) systems are crucial technologies for the realization of many of the benefits of healthcare ICT. Yet, the widespread adoption of electronic health records among hospitals has a "long road ahead" according to a report from the

Healthcare Financial Management Association (HFMA) of a 2006 survey of senior healthcare finance executives at hospitals and health systems and a roundtable discussion of healthcare finance executives. The report concludes that larger hospitals fare better in EHR adoption than mid-sized or small hospitals, and nonrural hospitals, slightly better than rural hospitals. The report also noted that EHR functions in which the greatest number of hospitals reported significant progress are order entry, results management, electronic health information/data capture, and administrative processes, with no much progress made with clinical decision support, health outcomes reporting, and patient access. According to the report, the lack of national standards and code sets is the most significant barrier in the way of adopting EHR nationally, with lack of available funding, next. It is hardly surprising then that healthcare organizations are emphasizing the need for the government to help facilitate standards and code sets development and provide grant funding and payment incentives to propel EHR adoption. The nationwide adoption of electronic health records would certainly be a significant step forward in improving healthcare delivery. Improvement in health services in turn would help improve the health of individuals in the country. Healthcare ICT would facilitate these processes, and would in so doing, help reduce healthcare costs, without compromising the quality of service delivery. We will explore these and other relevant issues further in this book, at the end of which it would be clear that promoting the widespread adoption of healthcare ICT requires the determined efforts of us all, who as stakeholders in healthcare delivery, must ensure that it is, and remains qualitative, accessible, and affordable for us, and for generations to come.

The Technology, Health, & Insurance Triangle

Progress in technology is helping the health industry achieve its goals of reducing health costs while simultaneously providing qualitative healthcare. One of the most critical benefits of healthcare ICT deployment is in facilitating real time access to vital patient data and information at the point of care (POC). Wireless technology for example is increasingly important in this regard, which faster connections and wider broadband has made possible in recent times. Public expectations of healthcare services for example continue to be high. Technologies such as mobile and wireless are helping meet some of these expectations. Patients and their relatives for example can now watch television, listen to the radio and surf the Internet without having to leaving the emergency room (ER), and with regard to the patient, his or her ER bed, although such services fall under the non-clinical services that some recommend should attract user fees even in publicly funded systems. ER departments, for example that of the new $3.1-million 10,000-square-foot emergency care department Florida's Sun Coast Hospital, phase I of which it opened on January 17, 2006, now offer a variety of wireless-based valued-added services to their clients. The Hospital's Patientline, a computer/television terminal that allows patients to check e-mail, use the phone, and to watch television, typifies the meaning of consumer-driven healthcare, which increasingly more healthcare stakeholders now embrace. When operational in full, the facility would offer even more technology-enabled services. Physicians would be able to review lab work results and other patient information on the computer screen, and patients able to get on the Internet via wireless network connections in the waiting room while waiting to see the doctor. Physicians could use a computer terminal in each patient room to access patient medical records and view lab results or do so via their mobile devices; emergency room staff would be able to use the wireless network to sign in patients more proficiently and speed up patients' access to doctors. With the new wireless technologies, ER staffers would be able to register patients at their bedsides, thereby reducing time spent waiting for that purpose in the waiting room. Generally, ER staffers take up to an hour to fill out paperwork for every hour of care. These new technologies would result in better time management: less time spent filling out forms, fewer patient record loss, and more effective service provision. Suncoast's paperless environment would also allow physicians to access digital X-rays from several workstations instead of having to look at the actual X-ray films. Its new ER would also have a new glass-enclosed waiting room where it would offer wireless technology to patients and their caretakers, enabling them to access the Internet on their personal digital assistants (PDAs) or notebooks, giving them something to do other than watch TV. What are the technologies behind these valuable functionalities? Intel officially launched its first WiMAX chipset, the Intel PRO/Wireless 5116 chip, termed Rosedale, on April 18, 2005. WiMAX means Worldwide Interoperability for Microwave Access. This people-friendly moniker for the IEEE 802.16 standard is the certification name, the standard best suited for delivering non-line-of-sight (NLOS) wireless broadband access to both fixed and nomadic users. Did the chip signal a new epoch of wireless broadband access? Some would say, may be not, as the 802.16-2004 standard or WiMAX received approval in 2004 but the equipment has to wait for interoperability testing. Furthermore, the mobile edition of the standard (802.16e) needs to wait even longer. Estimated commencement of certification for mobile WiMAX is mid-2006, when the certification labs open, with the first certified products available in the first quarter of 2007. Prior to then, WiMAX would have to vie with fixed broadband such as DSL, T1 and cable, with mobile devices such as notebooks and PDAs, also having to wait to be WiMAX-enabled. In other words, two important functionalities of WiMAX technologies for healthcare delivery portability, and mobility access, would have to wait, a key point that insurers and interested stakeholders need to know in developing their healthcare ICT strategy. Indeed, on 19 January 2006, the WiMAX Forum, an industry-led, non-profit corporation formed to promote and certify compatibility and interoperability of broadband wireless products, announced the first fixed wireless broadband network

17

products to achieve the designation of WiMAX Forum Certified. Revealed at the WCA Technical and Business Symposium in San Jose, the first companies and products to complete certification and interoperability testing, include Aperto Networks' PacketMAX 5000 base station, Redline Communications' RedMAX AN-100U base station, SEQUANS Communications' SQN2010 SoC base station solution, and Wavesat's miniMAX customer premise equipment (CPE) solution. The development of the products followed the WiMAX Forumdefined certification profile for 3.5 GHz systems, based on the IEEE 802.16-2004 and ETSI HiperMAN standards, each hardware system required to pass stringent and extensive test procedures, including protocol conformance, radio conformance and interoperability testing. WiMAX, designed for metropolitan area networks (MAN) has not replaced but complemented Wi-Fi, which stands for wireless fidelity, actually designed for local area networks (LAN) by extending its reach and providing a "Wi-Fi like" user experience but wider coverage. Between 2006-2008, both 802.16 (WiMAX) and 802.11(Wi-Fi) will be available in end user devices from laptops to PDAs, delivering wireless connectivity directly to the end user, stationary or mobile, when the health industry would be able to reap full benefits from these technologies. The new generation of 3G such as HSDPA and 1xEV-DO Rev A, are offering even more functionalities. Evolution Data Optimized (EV-DO) is a secure technology designed for service providers rather than the home and corporate environment. Code Division Multiple Access (CDMA)-based, it is a third-generation (3G) broadband wireless packet data technology, optimized for high-speed mobile data applications. EV-DO is already providing fully mobile wireless broadband services, also has speed advantage, and has wider coverage and superior network economics than Wi-Fi or WiMAX. Eavesdropping is also unknown with CDMA-based voice systems, unlike seen with several other wireless voice technologies, and EV-DO standard offers several levels of access control or authentication. Nonetheless, Wi-Fi clouds are increasingly gaining currency in many cities, although there are questions regarding the efficiency of this technology. Meanwhile the Bluetooth Special Interest Group and Ultrawideband developers have collaborated to resolve the incompatibility of their wireless networking technologies. Some of these incompatible networking technologies include Zigbee, Wi-Fi, Ultrawideband, Bluetooth, and Near Field Communications. By making these technologies compatible, developers and end user alike would be able to enjoy the high transfer rates of the Ultrawideband technology on a variety of devices that use Bluetooth such as mobile phones and other handheld devices, which are becoming more commonly sued in the health industry. This was a major boost in transfer speed as Ultrawideband speeds range between 100 megabits and 200 megabits over a range of 10- to 20-feet. The decision to make these technologies compatible would facilitate the evolution of digital media, among other benefits, and augurs well for profitability as some SIG members such as Motorola and Intel, also have major stakes in Ultrawideband specifications. Bluetooth consumes little power hence better suits mobile phones whereas Wi-Fi has a broader spectrum but needs more battery power. Faster transfer speeds make it easier for end users to send and receive data with any of these devices. While experts are already predicting the development of products capable of using the combined technologies, progress continues apace with new technologies, for example, impulse-radio ultra-wideband (IR-UWB), which may result in self-organizing wireless personal area networks, emerging. According to researchers working under the Information Society Technologies (IST), project Ultra-wideband Concepts for Ad-hoc Networks (UCAN,) who recently developed a complete UWB system, UWB is useful for communication, ranging, and localization, works up to 10 meters, with ranging accuracy up to 15 centimeters in line of sight. Impulse-radio UWB is superior to other short-range wireless technologies, which, for example, Bluetooth, utilizes more power and cannot do localization. Radio frequency identification (RFID) has a very short range, most applications utilizing uniquely the passive tags, without batteries. Because impulse-radio UWB spreads energy over the bandwidth at low peak power, it would not conflict with other short-range technologies. UWB, based on Direct Sequence Spread-Spectrum (DSSS) modulation, promoted mainly by Freescale focuses on two sorts of application in the short-range IEEE 802.15 technologies: low-range, high-throughput (IEEE 802.15.3a) and low power, low-complexity/sensor networks (the 802.15.4a version). There is little doubt that these technologies would play an increasing role healthcare delivery particularly with the current emphasis on ambulatory and domiciliary care. Health insurers need to appreciate the effects emerging technologies would have on their operations, including on billing for services provided by doctors and other healthcare professionals, via devices such as mobile phones and PDAs.

Technology is just one aspect of the multiplicity of factors impinging on the health industry that would directly or other affect the health insurance industry. Yet, it is one the underlines many of the new concepts that are changing the healthcare delivery landscape. In his 2006 State of the Union speech, the US President, George Bush reaffirmed his commitment to providing Americans with electronic health records (EHR). The President stated that government "will make wider use of electronic medical records and other health information technology to help control costs and reduce dangerous medical errors". These objectives reflect two of the major concerns that the health industry, in collaboration with the health insurance industry must address, and healthcare ICT could indeed, help in achieving these goals. The President also stressed the need for the US to eschew isolationism, which suggests that the country is willing to operate in the global arena, including in the global health arena, collaborating with other countries in tackling problems common to all humankind that threaten its very existence, for example, an avian flu pandemic. In order to participate in the global health community, it has to take its own health seriously, which explain the President s proposals to invest more in healthcare ICT to meet the challenge of rising health costs, which by extension represents significant costs to business and industry as well. EHR is the bedrock of efforts to exploit the many benefits of healthcare ICT. Health insurance and other businesses have vested interested in supporting government efforts to implement nationwide electronic health information networks including EHR. These efforts do not just mean offering incentives to healthcare providers to implement healthcare ICT, including electronic medical records (EMR), but also promoting the acceptance of these technologies by the public, current efforts along which direction seem to be working. The public is not only increasingly embracing the idea of EHR; many are actually buying-in into the idea of online personal health records (PHR). Indeed, private organizations are emerging that provide Internet-based PHR services for individuals. The idea of PHR, despite concerns about privacy and confidentiality seems increasingly attractive as it provides individuals some measure of control over their personal health information, the information only accessible to the individual and those that they authorized. MyMedicalRecords.com, one of such companies noted that healthcare experts agree that reductions in healthcare costs that would result if every American had an electronic patient health record would be almost US$1000 billion yearly. Furthermore, by the combination of benefits of such records within a more pervasive EHR systems also reducing medical errors, morbidities, and mortalities, premiums would fall, businesses would have a more productive workforce, and health insurance firms would become more profitable. Indeed, collaborative efforts on patient formation already exists, exemplified by the formation of regional health information networks in the US, for example, recently by a group of physician practices, a hospital, and insurer, which formed the Integrated Physician Network Avista, in the Boulder, Colorado, area. The group's leaders include Clinica Campesina Family Health Services, a federally qualified medical center; Colorado Access, an insurer serving the medically underserved; and 14 private physician practices with 19 locations. The Regional Health Information Organizations (RHIO) concentrates on improving care for the uninsured and those not enrolled in Medicare and Medicaid. Participating physicians, 108 in all, will be able to access the same electronic health records (EHR) software, integrated with the Medical Information Technologies' information system of Avista Adventist Hospital. Indeed, the network also has just finished a laboratory interface with Quest Diagnostics. This is the emerging, technology-backed, healthcare milieu in the US. All the RHIOs in the country would link with the national health information network (NHIN), the development of prototypes for which, expected by the fall, 2006. RHIOs will have local flavors in terms of value-added service provision depending on the specific needs of the populations that they serve. However, the final objectives would be the same nationwide. RHIOs will support local stakeholders in some way, and as the NHIN prototypes take shape, may need to more or less modify their business models and market approaches so that they could participate well in the NHIN.

The Office of the National Coordinator for health information technology (ONC) in the US has four stated sequential goals as parts of its vision of the future of healthcare in the country, namely, informing clinicians, interconnecting them, personalizing care, and thus improving population health. These goals speak eloquently to the central role of healthcare ICT in the future of healthcare in the country. Indeed, as the ONC clearly states "Our fourth and final goal is the most challenging and far-reaching but also the most important-improving the health of the entire nation. This task cannot "":contemplated without timely and accurate information. But with a concerted and unified effort at all levels of government and private endeavor, a strong foundation for population health can be attained." The ONC thus reaffirms the need not just for healthcare ICT in meeting the objectives of population health, and albeit, all other goals it has set to achieve, but that for collaboration among stakeholders. The ONC further states, " To accomplish this ultimate goal, the federal government has proposed three primary strategies: unifying public health surveillance systems; streamlining quality and health status monitoring; and accelerating the pace at which scientific discoveries in medicine are disseminated into medical practice." The emphasis of the ONC on research and medical progress underscores the point that stakeholders, including the health insurance industry cannot afford to ignore developments in medical research and practice. In particular, with regard to the health insurance industry, medical knowledge is changing so rapidly that an insurer that failed to keep abreast of this changing knowledge risks compromising its competitiveness, and indeed, its very survival. To buttress the point that collaboration is key to getting any national health information network off the ground, Florida, awarded over $1.5 Million for EHRs in a recent announcement by its Lt. Governor Toni Jennings and Agency for Health Care Administration (AHCA) Secretary Alan Levine, joined by representatives of the Tampa Bay Regional Health Information Organization. The announcement named the recipients of the Florida Health Information Network (FHIN) grants on January 6, 2006, the grants designed to facilitate the adoption and use of privacy-protected electronic health records in the State. In 2005, the Florida Legislature appropriated $1.5 million to fund the development of the FHIN, and in 2006, the State Governor Jeb Bush will request $5 million in recurring funding for additional grants to support broadening the scope of EHRs. Also in the US, the Michigan Governor Jennifer M. Granholm, launched a Statewide Health Information Network, outlined in a three-step plan to bring healthcare delivery into the 21st century during her January 25 State of the State Address, chief among which is the use of technology, to improve the health system. According to the Governor, " In the future, you will be able to give your pharmacist, your doctor, or the emergency room immediate access to your information, but you will control who sees it and what it is used for. Think about it, never having to remember the name of the medicines you have been prescribed. Never having to fill out another form detailing your medical history, your allergies, and the last time your 10-year-old got a tetanus shot." Gov. Granholm also plans to introduce a new insurance product called the Michigan First Health Care Plan and public-private partnerships to promote a culture of physical activity, prevention, and wellness in the state. Do these plans not clearly indicate the focus of healthcare in the future? The private sector is also actively involved in promoting healthcare ICT. The Robert Wood Johnson Foundation (RWJF) in the US recently funded 21 grants, up to $100,000 each, to state and local health departments and public health institutes for 12-month projects, named InformationLinks, designed to quicken ICT use by state and local public health agencies.

While many governments recognize the need to invest in healthcare ICT,

financial constraints combined with the sometimes-substantial financial outlay some of these technologies demand threatens their widespread adoption. A report published in the Daily Mail on February 3, 2006 for example noted that the extra money pumped into the NHS in England in the next year would go into pay rises and increased drugs costs, according to an analysis by The King's Fund health think-tank. The think-tank analyzed data from the Department of Health. Specifically, it suggested that almost 40% of the £4.5 billion cash increase for hospital and community health services for 2006/07 would go into funding staff pay rises, an additional 32% of the extra money, into higher prices and increases in costs linked to recommendations by the National Institute for Health and Clinical Excellence (NICE), clinical negligence and capital costs. This means only 28% or about £1.26 billion left for other developments for example reducing waiting times and other Government priorities. Indeed, the briefing paper titled, "Where's the money going?" also noted that projected NHS deficit for the end of this financial year would be the largest since the Labor government came to power, the six-month projection, more than £500 million for 2005/06, expect to fall significantly by the end of the financial year. The Government has deployed its "turnaround teams" into 18 NHS trusts to assist in solving their financial problems, as John Appleby, King's Fund chief economist, noted, the new data clearly is an indication of the financial pressure the NHS currently faces. This situation is not peculiar to the NHS, and paradoxically, is one that healthcare ICT could help turn around. By helping to rationalize drug prescribing, reducing medical errors, enabling patients and doctors to discuss options including cost considerations, and indeed, by helping prevent illness in the first place, and reducing morbidities, healthcare ICT could significantly reduce drugs costs. It would be prudent therefore, to invest rather than not in order to turn the NHS financial difficulties around for example. Indeed, there should be increasing focus on various aspects of the applications of ICT in healthcare delivery, as for example the plan of the US federal advisory body to commence work on projects that range from strengthening the U.S. healthcare system's public health event monitoring network to enabling consumers to have access to personal health records (PHR.). The American Health Information Community (AHIC) concluded at its meeting on January 31, 2006 in Washington, D.C., will collate recommendations in a year including that of a biosurveillance work group that would enable within a year, sending ambulatory and emergency department data in a standardized, de-identified format to public health agencies within 24 hours. AHIC also expects recommendations from a chronic care work group that will explore how widespread use of secure messaging could help clinicians and patients communicate. It also expects suggestions from a consumer empowerment work-group on how to make a pre-populated, secure electronic registration summary available to certain populations, and on ways to make a medication history linked to the registration summary widely available within a year. AHIC also looks forward to ideas from an EHR work group on how to make standardized, current, and historical lab data available for clinical care. These conclusions reiterate the importance of collaboration of a wide variety of government and private organizations and individuals in seeking and implementing solutions to healthcare problems, including assuring the quality of healthcare delivery, and reducing soaring health costs, and in promoting healthcare ICT diffusion. There is no doubt that the recommendations of the various work groups, which also highlight the role newer technologies would play in health services delivery, would help in achieving these objectives. There is no disputing the fact many see the human factor increasingly as just as important as technological progress and capital accumulation, and indeed, other factors, in economic development. This explains the increasing appreciation of the concept of population health, which many governments are making a priority and would become even more relevant in years ahead, which is inevitable if health is no longer simply the absence of disease and if we conceptualized overpopulation in realistic terms. In particular, we need not panic about medical progress reducing mortality and leaving fertility intact, as Winslow1 advised back in 1951 in his "Interrelationships of poverty and disease", in a World Health Organization (WHO) monograph that year. Debate over whether we should preserve health for those prior to or in the productive life stages, or put differently whether we should concern ourselves with present or future generations linger on, exemplified by arguments over age-weighted Disability-/Quality-Adjusted Life-year (DALY/QUALY) measurements. However, the acute realization of the economic devastation of HIV/AIDS[2] and Sen's[3] works on human capabilities have brought the idea of disease/death prevention as drivers of population efficiency , and from which human capital theory evolved in the 1960s squarely back to the fore. Far from conceptualizing human beings as means of production or simply in material terms, current concepts of sustainable development embrace the ideas of human aspirations, and development and what Winslow termed "man-with-nature", which provide the intellectual cobblestone of the quest to redress inequity and inequality in all aspects of our lives, including in healthcare delivery. The logical extension of this quest is the concept of population health, and indeed, a collaborative national, and international approach to health exemplified by the Sector-Wide Approach (SWAP), an agreement by developed countries, the International Monetary Fund (IMF), and the World Bank, and the recent financial commitment of several countries to a common global war against the avian flu menace. There is no doubt that investing in health could negate poverty in any society, and that healthcare ICT could help both developed and developing countries achieve this goal, albeit, with healthcare ICT strategies tailored to meet specific needs of each country, and within the context of its established institutions and infrastructure.

Regardless of whether a country's health system is insurance or tax-financed,

the ultimate goal should be for all its peoples to receive qualitative healthcare rooted in preventive health principles. In any case, the difference between them mostly pertains to ownership and operations of hospitals and other healthcare institutions, with private (companies, trusts, and organizations) ownership in insurance-financed healthcare systems, publicly owned in countries with tax financing, although there is some degree of private sector in ownership and operation of these institutions in some of these countries. The differences with regard financing are even less in reality, with insurance contributions based on income, and deducted when income taxes are. Private insurance also have equalization principles, although many query their effectiveness in many countries, for example the US, which explains why some welcome many of the proposals in President Bush's 2006 State of the Union Speech. For example, the idea of coupling bare-bones, high-deductible insurance policy with an account into which people can deposit money tax-free, which they could later use for medical expenses, giving individuals a greater financial stake in obtaining reasonably priced care, which by increasing competition, would force prices down, making healthcare more affordable, and many more individuals thus able to receive it. Indeed, proponents would argue, this would ultimately contribute to reducing the country's overall health costs. The president's plans would increase the annual amounts that people can contribute tax-free to their health savings accounts from the current maximums of \$2,700 for individuals and \$5,450 for families to \$5,250 and \$10,500, respectively, which proponents say would enable individuals to pay all of their out-of-pocket medical expenses tax-free. Some contend the accuracy of the estimates, and in particular, the idea of allowing payment for the premiums for the bare bones insurance policies with the tax-free funds, which they argue would deplete the latter leaving little if anything left, especially for poor families, to out-of-pocket medical expenses. A counter-argument would be why insurance premiums and indeed, out-of-pocket expenses, should be high in the first place. Just as shopping around for cost-effective treatment would force prices down, premiums are also subject to market forces. In fact, it is not always in the interest of insurance firms for premiums to be high, as they could still operate profitably with most clients being healthy, in which case, premiums would drop, or the insurer would soon be out of business. Here again, the value of disease prevention becomes clear, as is the role healthcare ICT could play in achieving it as rectifying information asymmetry, public health education, disease surveillance, and health promotion, among other public health measures predicate on the effective use of ICT. Insurers and healthcare providers have a major role to play in making the President's plans work, by making pricing and chargemasters, respectively available to the public, a measure that also implementing the appropriate healthcare ICT would facilitate. The President has proposed over the years the low-income tax credit, essentially that persons making up to \$15,000 and families, up to \$25,000 would be eligible for $1,000 and $3,000 credits, respectively, to assist in funding traditional comprehensive insurance, but in the new proposal, low-income families would only be eligible for the credit if they buy bare-bones policies. This new twist some would regard as inherently unfair to low-income earners but others would see as an attempt at equitable healthcare delivery by preventing abuse and overuse of tax credits, which could further escalate healthcare spending. Another proposed measure that is brewing controversy is preempting state regulation of insurance policies used to qualify for some health savings accounts, which the Federal government hopes would also help reduce the cost of policies by protecting them from costly state mandates. Although some believe the breaches federalism principles, some would argue it is the key to the success of the other proposals. Proponents would likely cite the Bush's administration recent extension of 60 days to the previous 30, for health insurers to provide beneficiaries of the Medicare prescription-drug plan benefits started on January 01, 2006, emergency supply of any drugs they were taking before the Medicare prescription drug benefit started as evidence that it is not necessarily on the insurers' side. The Department of Health and Human Services (HHS) noted that 60-day extension to the 30-day transitional coverage, required under the 2003 Medicare law, would allow beneficiaries more time to consider switching to less costly alternatives to their current medications, which as previously mentioned might eventually reduce overall health costs. With the observation of the HHS Secretary Mike Leavitt, that competition among private plans has led to lower costs under the new benefit, and that the Federal government will spend about 20% less per beneficiary in 2006 than previously estimated, and over the next five years, payments likely will be at least 10% lower than first estimated. Leavitt said that projected enrollment in the benefit has not changed significantly the plan seems to be yielding expected results. This is not to say that everything has been smooth sailing since January 01, 2006, as the Secretary in fact admitted initial difficulties implementing the plan, most observers have noted were administrative in nature, and due in the main to flawed ICT planning. This again underscores the central role that ICT plays in contemporary health insurance, and need for a well thought-out healthcare ICT strategy in order to achieve the objectives of the new health paradigm. Furthermore, insurers also have to wait out the outcomes of the lawsuits some states plan to file against the Federal government for alleged over-billing for the cost of prescription drugs for dual eligibles. At least 15 governors claim that this would result in their states spending more under the Medicare drug benefit through fiscal year 2006-2007 than they would have spent if they had continued offering prescription drug coverage to dual eligibles through Medicaid. California, for example, such extra costs to be $161 million by mid-2007, although the Federal government insists states would actually save money and that their calculations of losses overlooked the assistance that the federal government is providing for the costs of prescription drugs for state employees.

Clearly, the future of health insurance would depend on a combination of

factors least of which is government policy, reforms, and regulation. Healthcare costs would underpin many of these reforms and regulations, and healthcare ICT would play a leading role since it has the potential to reduce costs even if it takes some time for this to show. Also in the US, Medicare officials on February 02, 2006₄ said that the new prescription-drug benefit would cost taxpayers less than originally estimated, even, as mentioned earlier, some states are taking the Federal government to court over the program's costs, specifically for, as they claim, having to reimburse Medicare for more than they saved. States have to reimburse the Federal Medicare because the federal program provides drugs to some state Medicaid patients. Medicare officials indicated that cost estimates fell substantially in less than a month after the drug plan took off, the government's estimated 10-year cost dropping from $737 billion projected in 2005 to $678 billion, although still more than the initial $400 billion cost estimate. Premiums for persons that signed up for the program, an average of $25 a month, compared with $37 a month projected in July 2005, which officials credited to stronger-than-expected competition, itself due to lower drug costs. Could these projections change over the years, for worse for example, and could healthcare ICT not further reduce medication costs, hence premium costs, while in fact also improving the quality of healthcare delivery and ensure the changes are positive down the road? Would it still be necessary for the States threatening to sue the Federal government to actualize their plan considering that they would not have to reimburse the federal government as much for drugs used by the elderly and disabled already covered by Medicaid? These multfactorial influences are changing health insurance in other countries too. In Germany for example, hospitals customarily received their payments from social insurance funds based to the number of hospital days, which along hospital bed per population ration is much higher than for most other countries. In recent times, the health system in Germany is also under severe strain, due to rapidly increasing health costs, which the country is also seeking ways to reduce relying substantially on healthcare ICT. There is likely to influence competition among health insurers, which would have to depend paradoxically on healthcare ICT to enhance their value propositions in order to remain afloat. Competition is another key factor at play in healthcare delivery these days, even in countries with publicly funded health systems. This tendency strengthened, among others, after research studies comparing the UK NHS with Kaiser Health system in the US, which revealed consistently after adjusting for age distribution, the two healthcare systems provided similar health services at the same cost, but that the latter provided faster access to primary, hospital, and specialist care. Some contend that these findings support the need for competition and a free-market health system. While Kaiser Doctors cannot operate private practice, the organization competes in the private insurance-based US health system, and seems to be quite successful at doing so. Indeed, some studies showed that healthcare cost at Kaiser Permanente was less than half the average cost in the US. Success at Kaiser, which bears similarities with the UK publicly funded system, many claim results from their integration of finance and service provision, which of course, the implementation of the appropriate healthcare ICT underlie, a clear example of how such technologies could help reduce healthcare costs. Companies and other employers would likely play increasing roles in the health system, their decisions, likely to influence the health insurance industry substantially, as did those of Eastman Kodak and Xerox in Rochester, NY, in the 1990s. Some would argue that, the experiment, whereby the city at the companies' behest developed a healthcare system that essentially eschewed competition and embraced collaboration between insurers, failed. Others would hail the system's high-quality low cost healthcare, less than a third of the country's average, and that over 95% of the people had health insurance cover in the early 19990s. However, there were already threats to the systems. The role that some claim the emergent Medical Diagnosis-Related Group (DRG) system in the 1980s in the eventual demise of the experiment is arguable, but the lesson seems clear, that is, competition is essentially a survival game, the arena where costs issues ultimately play out. Interest in the application of ICT in healthcare delivery continues in different parts of the world. On February 03, 2006, in Brussels, European Health and Consumer Protection Commissioner Markos Kyprianou launched the "European Health Information Platform" or "Health in Europe" project. This health information system, co-financed with €1.4 million from the EU Public Health Program, and managed by the European Broadcasting Union (EBU), is a multimedia initiative aimed at creating a network of public broadcasters and other media in different countries in Europe. It also aims to foster the exchange of reports; including television documentaries, radio broadcasts, and press and internet articles on health issues, a key step toward rectifying the asymmetry of health information that is still rife, even in Europe. According to the Commissioner, "This partnership of TV and radio networks across Europe through the European Broadcasting Union will help keep citizens, and in particular patients and health professionals, informed on public health issues with a European dimension." The basis of Health in Health in Europe is an ongoing exchange of reports on health and medicine that TV broadcasters produce for their theme magazines, these reports, given rights-free to participating agencies, the times regularly reviewed. TV still being the medium of choice to reach the largest possible audiences in Europe explains its prominence but the Internet will also play a major role in the project. As individuals learn more about their health and about diseases and how to prevent them, they would likely be more open to embracing healthcare ICT, including being more willing to use personal health records and have their health information in electronic health records systems. Concerns about privacy in the

31

past have hampered progress with not only ICT diffusion but also regarding exploiting the benefits of technologies to the fullest. The Journal of Biomedical Informatics in September last year, for example reported such concerns were hindering efforts to spot disease clusters and monitor the health effects of environmental pollution, despite that data available to research groups investigating cancer clusters, for example is often restricted, altered or aggregated to ensure the privacy of individual patients. These measures, however, make it difficult if not impossible to conduct accurate geographical analyses of public health concerns, and may even lead to the use of misleading information in healthcare decisions. There is no doubt that this does not convince with the goals of population health. However, technological innovation could help solve this problem, although it is important to continue also to pursue confidence-building measures such as that rectifying current and preventing further information asymmetry could accomplish. New technology that uses software "agents" to explore data should provide healthcare professionals with more accurate and meaningful information yet protecting patients' identities, software programs able to set an explicit task, but then allowed the freedom to set goals and conduct operations required to actualize them, including being responsive to the environment and interacting and cooperating with other agents. Collaborating bodies could provide raw data for research in secure virtual milieu in which the gents could operate. These technologies would likely revolutionize public health research and programs, and help to identify the risk factors within our environment that we all face, and other health issues, in effect facilitating the achievement of the goals of population health.

Recent developments in Germany also typify the delicate interactions between technology, insurance, and health. The country has typically spent little on health healthcare ICT, just about 0.5% of its health expenditure, relative to other developed countries. However, this is changing, as the need for healthcare ICT continues to increase due to a combination of factors, namely, the shift in emphasis toward integrated healthcare ICT policy, which less than 20% of German hospitals currently embrace, the country's new reimbursement structures, and certain initiatives by government, among others. The country lagged behind other European countries in embracing integrated healthcare ICT partly because it hitherto lacked a coherent Federal eHealth focus, decentralization of healthcare administration resulting in wide variations and inconsistencies of healthcare ICT policies, strategies, and implementation, and increasingly tight health ICT budgets, among others. The change in emphasis would result in more investment in healthcare ICT aimed at integrating the hospital, and ambulatory care sectors of the German health system. The new country's new hospital billing system, based on diagnosis-related groups (DRGs) would also stimulate healthcare ICT investments and market growth. So would the healthcare reforms Acts promulgated in recently giving healthcare ICT priority status, and triggering Federal government plans to invest in a variety of healthcare ICT projects including e-prescriptions, electronic health records (EHR), personal health records (PHR), healthcare professional cards. The Health Ministry has recently released its master plan for "Information Technology Society Germany 2006," which emphasized that these projects would be at national, and not just at Länder levels, as in the past. The country also has new laws mandating digitalizing all patient information and procedure data going to the sickness funds for reimbursement. There are also new regulations regarding reimbursement for in-patient treatment post DRGs- introduction. Compliance with these regulations and laws require healthcare ICT investments many healthcare providers cannot afford to shun. In any case, many of these establishments are beginning to realize that that it is in their best interest to invest in healthcare ICT anyway because of increased awareness of its potential to streamline and improve their work processes, efficiencies, and productivity, cost-effectively. These developments are certainly going to make the healthcare ICT markets increasingly attractive to software and ICT vendors in the years ahead, certainly worth much more than the just over 1 billion Euro that it was three years ago, the estimated yearly growth for the clinical systems market, up to 20%, for the administrative systems markets, about 6%. Canada has a new

Conservative government that is committed to upholding the Canada Health Act. This means that the government would be against any measures provincial and territorial governments take that run counter to the Act, and has indicated its willingness to uphold the Act in its response to Alberta's latest private healthcare moves. Uncertainty looms over the country's health system considering the recent Supreme Court's decision to allow private healthcare in Quebec, and this would no doubt affect the pace and intensity of healthcare ICT investment in the country. There has been a significant increase in this regard in recent times, driven in the main by primary care reforms, including a stronger emphasis on population health. Healthcare authorities in the country are also eager to reduce wait times in hospitals across the country, and to contain spiraling healthcare costs, both of which there is consensus that healthcare ICT could help achieve. Canada has a large land mass and its population though concentrated along its southern strip, is also widely dispersed geographically, and with the country short of healthcare professionals has had little choice than to rely on the healthcare ICT, specifically, telehealth, to facilitate healthcare delivery to its peoples living in remote areas. The country has a long history of telehealth deployment. It would likely continue to utilize this means extensively in healthcare delivery in the years ahead. It would also likely to invest even more in healthcare ICT, over its $1.5 billion between 1997 and 2003, in its pursuit of qualitative healthcare delivery. By investing more in healthcare ICT, it would also hope to reduce its massive health spending, projected in 2005 at $142 billion, about 10.4% of the country's GDP (10.1% in 2004), the highest ever, according to data the Canadian Institute for Health Information (CIHI) released on December 07, 2005. Overall increase in health spending over 2004, 7.7%, and adjusted for inflation rate 5.5%. The Canada would witness a heightened interplay of the technology, health, and insurance trio, if private healthcare took off in earnest, particularly if the courts made similar rulings in other provinces as the Supreme Court did in Quebec. In this case, market forces would take over this tripartite situation with profound effects on each of its components and on the Canadian economy in general. Competition and collaboration would occur in various combinations among healthcare providers, healthcare ICT a major driver of these events. In other words, there would likely be proliferation of private healthcare providers, conventional and otherwise, all striving to outmaneuver their competition via technology-based value added services. It would then no longer be just going to one's GP and sitting, and just waiting. Some GPs might even have a playroom for their clients' children complete with X-Box and other computer games. Clients might be able to surf the Internet while they wait to see their doctors. GPs might have an adjacent wellness center equipped fully with the latest gadgets and perhaps tailored for different ages and gender. Many GPs would have to merge to survive, particularly in the face of stiff competition from home and abroad. Venture capitalists would likely be all over the country, building sophisticated specialist clinics equipped with the latest healthcare technologies. Meantime, the public health systems would have to buck up or wither away. There would likely be a spate of closure of hospitals, no longer financially viable, as government efforts shift toward ambulatory and domiciliary care, which, in keeping with its population health goals would increasingly become its forte. Government would also step in, albeit cautiously to ensure the smooth operations of this new free-health market, and to protect the interests, in particular, of those of its peoples that would still depend exclusively on Medicare, and those that use the private health system. These developments would likely require revisiting the country's overall social and welfare services policies, as well as pension reforms, and reimbursement systems for doctors and other healthcare professionals. With regard to the latter, any large scale, private healthcare operations in the country would likely further tip the balance of the distribution of healthcare professionals, necessitating novel approaches to recruitment and retention policies for these personnel cadres. In short, any dramatic changes to the country's present healthcare system would result in changes in several aspects of its policy domains in equal measure. It would likely take some time for Canadians to acclimatize to these changes, which incidentally, would likely be in their favor in the long term, as competition would likely have an aggregate effect of reducing the costs of health insurance premiums, and their out-of-pocket healthcare expenses, while they would receive improved quality healthcare to the bargain. These positive effects, however, may not be immediately obvious, but would with time. As previously noted, no one knows if this scenario would materialize. What is less uncertain is that even without the change-provoking effects of market forces, and if the country ran only a publicly funded health system, healthcare ICT would trigger major changes in health service provision in the country. Canadians expect much from their health system, particularly one on which their governments at Federal/provincial/territorial levels are spending such a sizeable chunk of the country's resources. These expectations, increasingly sophisticated as they are, would continue to drive the quest for improvements in healthcare delivery, for example, wait times reduction. This would necessitate continued and indeed, increased healthcare ICT investments, having become clear that these technologies could help improve healthcare delivery while saving costs.

P rivate health insurance would continue to create controversy hotbeds in

many countries, and its position would likely become increasingly tenuous within the trio, as changes in the other two, which are increasingly frequent and intense, would have far-reaching implications for the health insurance industry. Consider the seeming spread of the new UK "supersurgery" phenomenon to the US, with people seeking medical attention in their neighborhood grocery store these days, confident that they would save money by saving a trip to the ER, yet get expected results. According to press reports, many more stores, ranging for small-scale chains such as Bultez' local Hy-Vee to megamarkets such as Wal-Mart and Target, have begun trial runs with in-store medical clinics. Reports indicate that retailers are venturing outside their traditional domains into healthcare essentially to buoy foot traffic rather than an attempt to create a new revenue stream, but these forays seems sufficiently promising for America Online founder Steve Case to invest $500 million in a firm that purchases stakes in smaller firms that set up the clinics, Revolution Health Group. These clinics appear to be convenient and cost saving, hence would likely mushroom before our very eyes, but what does this portend for the insurance industry? Based on a simple business model, essentially a medical clinic that outside company operates, with staff mostly nurses and/or physician assistants, these clinics provide a limited range of rudimentary tests and treatments at a lower cost than a doctor's office. Would this phenomenon, which incidentally has a different origin in the UK, where it is part of a deliberate government effort to move health services into the community, spread to Canada and other countries? These in-store clinics, for examples Quick Care at the Omaha Hy-Vee; Revolution's RediClinic, and MinuteClinic, which has 70 clinics in CVS pharmacies, Target Stores and Cub Foods supermarkets, are different from the so-called "doc in a box" stand-alone clinics, also increasingly common in the US. With patients requiring no appointments and open after regular business hours, many believe that these clinics provide ready access to care and could be the only healthcare service portal in certain places where GPs are few or lacking, besides offering the convenience of seeking help for a troublesome cough while in the grocery, shopping. Another significant aspect of this phenomenon is that these clinics list the price of care on a message board, giving patients the opportunity to shop around for care, which would overall make treatments in these clinics, which run minimal overheads, competitive and affordable. Some of them accept insurance plans, and charge only the co-payments but others will not accept co payments but will their clients a detailed receipt for submission to insurance providers. Some criticize these clinics for disrupting the continuity of care, but the phenomenon provides another instance of the changing healthcare landscape, how it affects the health insurance industry, and the role that healthcare ICT could play in solving the problem of continuity of care that id of concern to its critics. It also highlights how market forces could also be forces of innovation and creativity. In this regard, one could expect this business model to grow, and become even more sophisticated, and with Wal-Mart for example, having thousands, of outlets all over North America, including Canada, what implications would such developments have not just for health insurers, but for government's efforts at human resource developments in both the medical and paramedical fields. Could this be an interim solution to the acute shortage of medical personnel in some countries, and in underserved areas of others? Would there be need for government to regulate practice in these clinics, and indeed, prices of care? Are there issues of certification involved? What are the prospects of even one malpractice suit literally putting an abrupt end to this phenomenon? The answers to these questions would likely be important concerning the future of this emergent health service model. Developments in medical research are also going to continue to influence health insurance as the following examples show. Insurers might have known for sometime that women with heart attacks do not have the same symptoms as men with the same condition do, but would results from the massive Women's Ischemia Syndrome Evaluation (WISE), which have at last provided evidence to explain why, have any effect on insurance policies for men vis-à-vis women? How would the fact according to WISE investigators that doctors are missing the diagnosis in up to three million women with coronary heart disease because of the differences in their clinical presentation compared to men influence insurers' risk evaluation? The results of the WISE studies, published in the supplement to the February 07 2006 issue of the Journal of the American College of Cardiology, explained that in women, plaque, the fatty substance that clogs arteries in individuals with atherosclerosis, spreads out widely throughout the vessels rather than as in men, accumulating in specific locations. This explains why some women whose angiograms, results of imaging exam to identify partial or total occlusion of coronary arteries, are normal, may be at high risk for ischemic heart disease or heart attacks. Women also tend to have a different and more severe form of vascular disease than men. They also tend to have blockages in the tiny feeder vessels in the heart and to have stiffer, more inefficient aortas, defects that also usually do not show in angiograms, overall reducing women's chances of receiving aggressive treatments, for example using tiny flexible tubes, termed stents to open up arteries. Because the chances of being undiagnosed and untreated are therefore high in women, they are at higher risks of their condition progressing to major heart attacks. Indeed, about 50% of American women do not know that heart disease is the number one cause of death among women, but studies such as WISE is likely to change this under-recognition of the risks that they face with heart disease. Should the fact that also in the US, more than 250,000 women each year die from ischemic heart disease or related conditions, this number expected to rise with the graying of the population concern the insurance industry? Would the increasing awareness of these risks by women increase the numbers of them signing up for health insurance? Harvard researchers reported in the February 01, 2006 issue of Circulation: Journal of the American Heart Association, that cardiovascular disease causes 1 in 2.6 deaths in women and according to the US Centers for Disease Control and Prevention (CDC,) 38% of deaths in women compared to 22% for all cancers. Should the health and insurance industries, and other healthcare stakeholders not become more aggressive in health education campaigns alerting women to these risks? What role could healthcare ICT play in effectively getting the word out? Also in Circulation, Harvard researchers reported that obesity is a significantly greater risk factor for heart attacks than a sedentary life style in women. Furthermore, studies also showed that increasing exercises without losing weight does not significantly reduce the risk, but that both do, and is the best way to reduce the risk. Regarding exercise, University of Texas researchers reported recently that a half hour exercise could improve mood in men and women suffering from clinical depression, and is a useful adjunct to conventional therapy for the condition, and British researchers concluded in a recent report that spontaneity often works when quitting smoking. What would insurers make of a recent research study in Taiwan published in the January 31, 2006 issue of the Canadian Medical Association Journal that showed that tallness is not always advantageous, at least for individuals suffering form diabetes? The researchers showed that tallness is an independent predictor of lower extremity amputation in such persons, which means that they should have closer monitoring for peripheral sensory loss and leg ulcer. Do these research findings not indicate influence that developments in healthcare, particularly advances in medical knowledge could have on the operations of this insurance industry? Furthermore, do they not highlight the interdependence of the trio of technology, health, and insurance in contemporary health affairs? In particular, these examples, underscore the need for health insurance firms to be cognizant of recent medical findings, which could make a significant difference to their evaluation of actuarial risks and pricing policies. It could also help them determine the areas that they need to focus on in future value propositions.

Health insurers could offer their clients wellness programs for example tailored to specific age groups, gender, or disease category, as part of their value-added services. Incidentally, according to CDC, the prevalence of obstructive coronary artery disease is relatively low among premenopausal women, and women generally do not catch up to men in rates of coronary artery disease until they are in their 70s. Doe this mean that women should ignore the risks mentioned earlier? Certainly not, because in the first place, they could have a heart disease well before the seventies, and considering the risks of missed diagnosis, could be in grave danger without treatment of the condition. Indeed, both women and men should recognize the fact that the best way to prevent heart disease, is via exercise and weight loss. No one should wait until the seventies to take this advice to heart, and act on it. With new technologies developed at what some would consider a frenetic pace, opportunities abound, made possible by healthcare ICT to exercise and trim down suited to individual needs and abilities. For example, an elderly person of seventy might not be able to tolerate the physical demands of an exercise regime that a younger person would not find little tasking. Individuals also require different exercise levels based on their health condition, for example, if they have an underlying, even if non-cardiac, disease. Healthcare technologies would help address these peculiar circumstances successfully. The delivery of qualitative healthcare in our times has become imperative. Nonetheless, this must be within certain constraints, chief of which is budgetary. Again, the implementation of the appropriate healthcare ICT would facilitate the achievement of these goals. Because of their close ties with health insurance, the there is no disputing the link between the survival of any of them to that of the trio.

References

1. Interrelationships of poverty and disease. In. Winslow C-EA. *The cost of sickness and the price of health*. Geneva: World Health Organization; 1951. WHO Monograph Series, No. 7, Chapter 4.

2. Bell, C Devarajan S, Gersbach, H. *The long-run economics of AIDS: theory and an application to South Africa*. Washington (DC): The World Bank; 2003. Policy Research Working Paper 3128.

3. Sen, A. Health in Development. Bull World Health Organ 1999; 77: 619-23

4. Available at:

http://www.usatoday.com/printedition/news/20060203/a_medicare03.art.htm
Accessed on January 03, 2006

ICT & Workers' Health

Workers'wages are growing leisurely, and in fact, many are losing their jobs, as many as 30,000 at Ford Motor Co alone recently. Many that have jobs and should have retired are staying on if they could, some for as long as a decade, because they cannot afford health insurance. School districts are running bankrupt because they can no longer service the generous retirement packages erstwhile strong teacher unions negotiated, particularly in states such as California. To complicate matters for teachers, strict new accounting rules threaten to mandate school districts to fund their benefits either now or essentially never. The US spent 16% of its Gross Domestic Product (GDP), about US$1.9 trillion on health in 2004. The US may have the distinction among developed countries of being the only one tax-subsidized employer-based insurance fund a significant percentage of healthcare insurance, yet the state pays invariably about half of country's health bill. Let us break down the figures. 174 million Americans have employer-based health insurance. 27 million have self-paid, health insurance with no tax subsidy. Government via Medicare sponsors 40 million elderly and disabled citizens, via Medicaid, with both federal and state government involvement, 38 million poor Americans, leaving 46 million Americans uninsured, although many by choice. Despite its enviable strengths, for examples, patients having a variety of choices of health services, the large numbers of uninsured Americans, the high healthcare costs, and inconsistent quality of services, are huge setbacks for the country's health system relative to those of other developed countries. In particular, healthcare spending has mostly surpassed income growth averagely by 2.5% points annually save for the mid-1990s when negotiated discounts with doctors by Health Maintenance Organizations (HMOs) and subsequent health service restrictions slowed health inflation, which though soared again a few years later with public outrage against the HMOs and resultant political repercussions. This increasing health inflation rate, which is much greater than inflation in general, is partly responsible for companies reducing health insurance coverage for their workers, and many increasing co-payments and deductibles, and health insurance for retirees. It is increasingly clear that companies are struggling to cope with the burden of their health insurance commitments, or better still, employers in general. School districts for example, have been coping fairly well over the years, and have not considered it imperative to address the problem of health insurance for their retirees. This was partly because health costs were reasonably steady and retirement health plans made it easy to offer their workers a precious benefit with no need to pay more money for higher salaries. Many benefits packages still pledge lifetime benefits, but negotiations that brought them into being clearly little anticipated the high costs they would incur down the road. This now burden expense is crippling many a school district today, to a larger or smaller extent. A 2004 study by the Citizens Research Council of Michigan showed that the state's cost of providing retiree health care could be as high as almost 20 cents of every dollar spent on payroll by 2020. This would be over thrice its cost in 2004. In short, and as is happening with American companies, schools with a graying workforce, now have to seek ways to reduce healthcare costs, and as for companies, healthcare ICT could help achieve this goal. Workers assured of generous lifetime benefits for themselves, and spouses, in the bygone days when unionism was at its zenith, are now discovering that the promises they received are anything but certain. In Fresno, an audit sponsored by local business leaders in 2005 showed that the school district, despite dwindling enrollment and tax support, was paying $24 million on free lifetime health benefits to employees' dependents, including spouses and offspring. The audit estimated all its existing retiree health commitments at $1.1 billion, which is more than its total budget, although still much less than the estimated $5 billion amount for the Los Angeles school district, the second-largest school district in the country. Fresno may have a lid on payment, but resolving teachers' benefits issues is taking new dimensions, including the involvement of the Supreme Court, which in Minnesota in 2005 ruled against taking away after retirement, benefits teachers and other public employees won through collective bargaining. A combination of increasing costs, and numbers of retirees, are the main factors creating the financial crisis for school districts, although some of them have also had poor returns on their investments. The clamor for reform is rife, including the introduction of an audit of retiree health care systems to account for current and future costs, failure to do which could affect the district's credit ratings. The new Government Accounting Standards Board guidelines took effect on January 01, 2006. Would this help, some would ask, or should retirees give up and simply stay healthy? The truth of the matter is that employer-provided health coverage for retirees, previously common, is dying out. On February 08, 2006, General Motors (GM) announced that it plans to cap its health care spending for salaried retirees at 2006 levels starting in 2007, part of an overall saving effort by the company, which includes slashing its stock dividend by half and reducing executive compensation. This plan means that retirees would have to fund future health care cost increases, thus paying higher monthly premiums, deductibles, and prescription medication bills, after reaching the limit. The plan will affect about 100,000 salaried retirees and 26,000 current employees hired before 1993, salaried employees hired after 1993 not eligible for retiree health coverage. The company hopes to reduce future health care liabilities by $4.8 billion and save $900 million in yearly administrative costs, estimated total cash savings in five years, about $200 million, including $1.7 billion in immediate savings. This plan results from an agreement with United Auto Workers Union (UAW) in 2005, to trim union workers' health benefits. GM lost $8.6 billion in 2005, and spent $5.4 billion on health care costs and prescription drugs on its 1.1 million employees, retirees and dependants, during the same year. Indeed, problems relating to health benefits for retirees not only affect the finances of many other companies in the US, regardless of industry, it is in fact, compromising their competitiveness, industry analysts argue. The question then is, how many more companies would lay workers off in order to straighten out their finances, and is this the way out for these companies? What could the consequences of these layoffs be for workers and their families, and for the country's overall health? What could the backlash be for the companies themselves, and for the nation's sustainable economic development? Could healthcare ICT help solve or at least

44

attenuate these problems? Many analysts think that GM's financial woes are multifactorial in origin, and not just due to health benefits, and that the company needs to tackle these other problems too, for example the rising costs of materials used in the manufacturing processes. No one doubts though that the three-fold inflation rate in health care costs in the country also is a significant factor. Could healthcare ICT not help reduce these costs, and if so, the healthcare costs of companies, and would it then still be necessary to retrench workers? It is not only employers that feel the burden of health benefits, with the public sector paying close to 60% of the US healthcare bills, via Medicare, Medicaid, veterans healthcare, and tax subsidies, a percentage that will likely increase with companies cutting-down on health spending and baby-boomers retiring. Some experts believe that federal health spending would be twice its percentage of the economy by 2020, which would almost certainly warrant tax increases. Experts agree that urgent action needs taken to forestall the possible dire consequences for US healthcare of the current trends of rising government healthcare spending and increasingly limited coverage that companies seem willing to provide. However, to find solutions, one needs first know the causes of a problem, which experts believe boil down to the country's imperfect health markets. Some of the problems contributing to this imperfection include remuneration issues, information asymmetry, tax subsidies for employer-purchased health insurance, lack of incentives, slow healthcare ICT diffusion, and high rates of malpractice suits, among others. From fee-for-service, that some claim encourages doctors to perform unnecessary procedures, to Americans paying only one-sixth on the average on healthcare from their own resources, to high tax subsidies for employer-purchased insurance promoting costly healthcare, and the epidemic of malpractice suits that encourage defensive medicine, consensus on many of the ills of the US health system is not lacking. However, there is precious little agreement on the best approaches to addressing these problems. Fix an imperfect market or accept it is unfixable and go for heavy regulations? Revamp the health system in one fell swoop or go slow? There would always be proponents on either side of the debate on whither the US health system. Some would argue however, that Capitol Hill abhors radical change, and would rather broaden coverage than control costs, although States, at least some for example, Maryland with its so-called "Wal-Mart Bill" mandating employers with over 10,000 workers to spend 8% of their payroll on health insurance, are unabashed about being radical. Incidentally, a national retail-industry trade association is challenging the law in a suit filed on February 08, 2006 and announced in Arlington, Va., by the Retail Industry Leaders Association (RILA), which represents companies that operate more than 100,000 stores with more than $1.4 trillion in annual sales. The Washington State legislature has also introduced a bill that would compel large firms, including Wal-Mart, to pay a minimum amount for health benefits for their workers1. Long Island's Suffolk County passed its own version last fall, mandating the setting aside of $3 on healthcare for each hour a worker is on the job. The legislative encounters in 30 states clearly point to healthcare accessibility garnering political traction, which has some wondering whether this law, based on what some term the fair share rule, is the panacea for the problems of America's uninsured workers, or indeed those of the entire health system. Even if such laws were the prerogative of the US Federal rather than state or local government as RILA, which seeks to annul the Maryland and Suffolk County laws is currently arguing in court, would they bale the country's health system out of its current doldrums? As some contend, would the laws not simply worsen the country's unemployment situation, as there could be much less funds for creating jobs, rather than broaden health care coverage? The US health system is heavily employer-based, although 16 percent of Americans, about 45 million, do not have health insurance, most of who incidentally live in households with at least one full-time worker. Some argue that the problem really is not with the large companies, most of which already offer health insurance to their workers, and that efforts should focus on the small businesses to offer health insurance. Most agree though that many workers in the large companies end up on Medicaid, or pile up unpaid hospital bills, for ER and sundry treatments, costs other clients end up paying somehow. In the US, the average that companies spent on health per employee in all industries in 2003 was $5,600, and $4,800 by retail/wholesale companies, although many companies spent much less than these averages. Furthermore, many companies are allegedly making their workers spend increasingly more on health from their pockets with higher deductibles and co-payments, and indeed, the proportion of employers offering health benefits has been falling progressively in recent times. So then, are the fair share laws, necessary? Some would say yes, even if they only make those companies not doing much regarding workers health insurance to start doing so, although others might insist that 8% does almost nothing for the uninsured, most of who earn very little anyway. Regardless of one's position, it is unlikely that anyone would disagree, that something needs done to solve the various problems relating to workers health benefits.

With increasingly more "pay-for-performance" initiatives operational in the country, whereby physicians and hospitals receive incentives based on the quality of services delivered, with payments adjusted on this score, there are indications that the health industry itself might lead the way in radically reforming the health system. Incidentally, healthcare ICT plays a central role not just in improving the quality service delivery, but also in performance evaluation, and ultimately in reducing healthcare costs. Consider the issue of patient safety, for example. A recent study published in the December 14, 2005 issue of the Journal of the American Medical Association [2], that surveyed over 100 hospitals in Missouri and Utah to assess progress made regarding improving patient safety from 2002 to 2004, found that although there was improvement in patient safety, it was incredibly modest. Yet, patient safety has been a topical issue in health care since the Institute of Medicine (IOM) estimated in 1999 that medical errors cause between 44,000 and 98,000 deaths annually in the US, the eighth leading cause of death, more than motor vehicle accidents, breast cancer, or AIDS. It is also, no doubt a significant cause of morbidity, and the country's rising healthcare costs. These disquieting statistics led many hospitals and health-care organizations to pledge to accelerate safety improvements, the adequacy of which this study has apparently raised doubts about. While the study did not paint a comprehensive picture of the safety improvements instituted across the country, and there is no doubt that some of the measures by hospitals in different parts of the country deserve commendation, much needs done to improve patient safety, and healthcare ICT could play a key role in doing so. For example, surgeons and anesthetists could discuss anesthesia risks, and other pertinent issues regarding an imminent surgical procedure with patients and their families before the surgery via Internet-based video feed. Patients could view this online or download and view it as many times as they wish, and in the comfort of their homes, and the reassuring presence of their families. Because patients do not have to come to the hospital for this purpose, it is one approach to resource optimization, human and material, with substantial cumulative costs savings to the bargain. Surgeons could also confirm which side of the body they should operate on and mark the site before witnesses prior to the operation itself. Doctors could order medications, lab tests, and radiological investigations electronically, avoiding error-prone paper prescriptions and physician order sheets. Despite its benefits in reducing medical errors, which many studies have confirmed[3], the above-mentioned study noted that just over two-thirds had implemented such computerized physician order entry (CPOE) for laboratory work or radiology in 2004, a little more than in 2002. For medication orders, the percentage of fully computerized hospitals was 34% in 2004, a less than 1% increase over the 2002 figure. In recognition of the need for patient safety, particularly following the 1999 IOM report, the California Senate passed a bill mandating urban hospitals to implement, by January 2005, a plan to reduce medication errors, addressing "technology implementation, such as, but not limited to, computerized physician order entry."[4] Some private organizations, notably the Leapfrog Group, comprising a number of large employers, have in fact tied CPOE implementation to some form of incentive for hospitals. "The Business Round Table (BRT)", which announced this program, and called it the Leapfrog Group, on November 15, 2000, also released new research indicating that CPOE, evidence-based hospital referral, and ICU staffing by physicians trained in critical care medicine could save up to 58,300 lives and prevent up to 522,000 medication errors each year[5]. The BRT actually stated that it was "encouraging employers to take safety "leaps" forward with their employees, retirees and families by rewarding the hospitals that implement significant safety improvements". Would healthcare costs have dropped had hospitals heeded this offer? Is it too late doing so? Besides reducing the chances of medical errors, as the overall weight of evidence has so far shown, because CPOE changes the ordering process, it could substantially optimize service utilization, decreasing the overuse, and misuse of health care services, thus reducing costs. By fostering compliance with evidence-based guidelines and practices, it further reduces the risks of medical errors, thus reducing the rates of illnesses arising thereof, minimizing the need for unnecessary hospitalizations, and shortening the lengths of hospital stays in others, and with hospital costs making up a significant chunk of healthcare costs, the savings in overall health costs could be remarkable. Therefore, CPOE just does not enhance performance and the quality of health services it does so cost-effectively. Indeed, in its 2000 announcement, BRT, specifically stated that members " of The Leapfrog Group have set out to reduce preventable medical errors by changing the way they purchase health care," according to Dr. Suzanne Delbanco, Ph.D., Executive Director of The Leapfrog Group. She added, "By encouraging health care providers to adopt three proven safety measures, thousands of Americans can be protected from disability and death." The three measures are CPOE, shown to reduce medical errors by 50%, and eviden ce-based hospital referral, and ICU staffing by physicians trained in critical care medicine, shown to reduce patient s risk of dying by over 30% and 10% respectively. Of course, significant barriers to the implementation of CPOE and these other measures exist, and include, besides costs, the reluctance of physicians to change current practices, misgiving about the possible benefits, and increased front-end time to enter orders. CPOE costs, including those of technology and organizational process analysis and redesign, system implementation and maintenance, updates and upgrades, quality evaluations and assurance, and of user training and support, among others could be substantial, but do the overall benefits of the technology in human and material terms not far outweigh these costs? Should healthcare organizations see CPOE and other healthcare ICT such as Radio Frequency Identification (RFID) and bar coding, the former, which obviates the need for line-of-sight on which the latter depends, pharmacy systems, electronic medical records (EMR), which present critical patient information at the point of care (POC), and event monitors, as critical tools for improving health care quality? The Missouri and Utah survey mentioned above also found hospitals lacking concerning another major safety issue, namely the long work hours of professional staff. There is little doubt that sleep-deprived hospital staffs, for example, resident doctors, are more error-prone. Yet, less than half the hospitals surveyed had a fully implemented policy to ensure doctors prescribing medications worked no longer than 12 consecutive hours. Here again, healthcare ICT could help. Increased workloads, which could be insidious or sudden, for example due to long wait lists, or an outbreak of some disease, respectively, shortage of healthcare personnel, and maldistribution of healthcare professionals, are some of the reasons for doctors working long hours, all issues that the use of appropriate healthcare ICT could help resolve. These problems also call for a deep exploration of the other relevant factors, for example, healthcare professionals' recruitment and retention policies, including incentives to attract physicians to rural and remote areas, remuneration policies, the use of physician assistants, research and development policies to encourage technological creativity, and indeed, the country's micro-and macro-economic policies. There needs to be more research efforts on more cost-effective delivery of health services to remote areas, for example. However, efforts in this direction should incorporate progress in medical knowledge, including changing patterns of disease prevalence, the country's health indicators, and the influence of demographic changes on approaches to disease prevention and treatments. Should there be more investments on tele-health for example? If so, on what aspects of tele-health should the focus be? Should it be on education, consultation, monitoring, or treatment or a combination of any of these? Would education not be important to prevent diseases, but would the education program be to prevent Malaria in Alaska? Would the need for tele-health consultation, treatment, and monitoring of diabetes not be higher among populations known to be at risk for the condition, notably Blacks and Hispanics? This sort of careful determination of resource utilization, including healthcare ICT deployment, based on solid evidence would result in significant cost-savings. However, it would also help ameliorate the problems of shortage of professionals, and improve the quality of healthcare delivery. It would be far-sighted for example for developed countries to consider the full ramifications of an aging population in deploying financial and technological resources. Indeed, such considerations are important in the current push of many of these countries toward ambulatory and domiciliary healthcare. Countries need to consider all the important factors at play in their health systems, and come up with novel and innovative ideas, if their goals of delivering qualitative health services without emptying their treasuries were to materialize. In Canada, Quebec is lately pursuing a new healthcare delivery model called complementarity. The idea is to concentrate the practice of some medical or surgical specialties in either of Montreal's two mega-hospitals, the MUHC and the CUSM. By concentrating expertise and certain care types in a single hospital, Quebec would be centralizing equipment, optimizing the effectiveness of the clinical teams, creating centers of excellence, and reducing overall healthcare costs. Some quarrel with the obvious costs of moving equipments, and clinical teams, but what about the long-term benefits in terms of cost savings for Quebec, and also in having centers of excellence that could attract clients from all over the world, generating revenues for the province that could help offset its rising healthcare costs? Some have also commented on the impact that such a plan would have on the training of doctors in the province. Do doctors currently have all their clinical rotations in one hospital? Would it not in fact enhance their appreciation of team dynamics for them to rotate through specialties in different hospitals, and with different clinical teams, perhaps with different institutional cultures? Would training in a center of excellence not encourage specialization and research, and perhaps spurn new medical knowledge if not even discoveries? Is this not what we need to move medical evolution forward at the pace appropriate for an age of increasing consumer expectation of health services, soaring healthcare costs, and in tandem with the intense pace of technological progress? With regard access to healthcare, such a plan would inevitably result in some hospitals becoming financially unviable, and would have to shut down. However, there is unlikely to be a mass closure of hospitals without adequate measures taken not to contradict the provisions of the

Canada Health Act, which guarantees accessibility to health services for all. Besides, the reality of contemporary and future healthcare is the need to provide qualitative services cost-effectively. Part of achieving this objective involves preventing illnesses and diseases in the first place, in keeping with the paradigm shift toward population health, which healthcare ICT is crucial in helping achieve. Another is acknowledging the reality of the direction healthcare delivery is going, particularly in the developed world, namely the push toward ambulatory and domiciliary health services, in which again, healthcare ICT has to play an active role for the successful implementation of such services. Perhaps the Quebec government also has the changing dynamics of healthcare delivery in mind following the recent Supreme Court decision to allow its peoples to patronize private health services. With its constitutional duties to provide healthcare to its peoples in accordance with the Canada Health Act looming large, the expectations of its peoples to receive comprehensive and accessible healthcare increasingly sophisticated, and its health spending relentlessly on the rise, could the province afford not to be competitive in the face of an imminent private health sector "invasion"? Indeed, the Quebec example should point the way to other Canadian provinces if only regarding generating "out-of-box" ideas on how to reduce their rising health spending while ensuring the delivery of qualitative health services in a rapidly changing socio-economic milieu, even if the Supreme Court ruling does not apply to them. The first for-profit medical facility, the Copeman Healthcare Center, is operational in Vancouver, for example, and heading eastward, with plans to open three such centers in Ontario by the end of summer, 2006. Also in 2006, the company plans to have outlets in Victoria, Calgary, Edmonton, Regina, Saskatoon, Winnipeg, Montreal, and Halifax, and according to its management, there is a lot of interest to join the company by physicians. The company insists that it is operating within the ambit of the Canada Health Act, and that its clients would still be receiving the insured services their provincial health plans offer. The company adopts a customer-driven approach to care, stressing the provision of qualitative services, including follow benchmarked protocols, and regular practice audits, and offering doctors generous paychecks. Is this the emerging reality of healthcare delivery in

Canada? Would many such centers spring up, perhaps some from even below the 49th parallel down the road? How would all this finally play out for workers and their families, and indeed, for all the peoples of Canada? Would provincial health services have to take a cue from Quebec and develop their own models, best suited to their respective needs, with all the relevant factors duly considered? Maybe, they would, maybe not. The London Free press reported in its February 10, 2006 edition that Ontario doctors are committed to a great public health care system accessible to all but also interested in improving it, according to the president of the Ontario Medical Association, Dr Greg Flynn, speaking in London. Dr Flynn reportedly also noted that the public appreciates that there are problems that considering how other countries deliver health care warrant, and that it is time to consider alternatives "at the edges" of the country's health system to control costs and offer patients more treatment options6. What role would healthcare ICT play in the competitiveness of either the public or private health system in this new dispensation? Would this quest for competitive edge ultimately reduce health spending, yet provide more accessible and high quality healthcare for more workers and their families, and would it help companies in reducing health benefits for retirees? What would be the overall effects of these developments on a country's future prosperity, in particular in its ability to achieve sustainable economic growth? German carmaker Volkswagen announced February 10, 2006, that it is set to hack 20,000 jobs in a restructuring bid that will run until 2009, the cut expected at its core Volkswagen business, and its shares hiked 8% to 54.79 euros, following the announcement. As with car manufacturers everywhere, these are trying times with competition on the rise, as are raw material costs and consumers reluctant to buy new models. Also in Europe, Renault has adopted a new strategy. Volkswagen wants to adjust production capacities and to use early retirement and voluntary redundancy packages as much as feasible, presumably to sustain its reported preliminary net profit of 1.1bn euros (£752m) for 2005, which surpassed analyst estimates, and total sales of 95.3bn euros in the same period. Indeed, the company expects sales and operating profit to increase in 2006. It is not difficult to see the short-and long-term implications for the country's health and economy that the company is slashing jobs in its bid to improve efficiency and cut costs. In a country where workers used to earn some of the highest pays in Europe, and receive some of the most generous benefits, many believe that German unification in 1991 marked the start of problems in the German economy. With unemployment rate at 11.6%, and 4.76 million unemployed, according government statistics, and nearly 40% of the unemployed, about 1.8 million out of job for over one year, that in September 2005, Volkswagen agreed to build a new sports utility vehicle in Germany only after unions agreed to wage concessions is understandable. Nonetheless, it did not stop the company from sending thousands of workers into the labor market. The economic reform packages of erstwhile Chancellor Gerhard Schroeder included cutting unemployment and welfare benefits and rolling them into one, in an attempt to compel people to discard what the Germans call the "soziale Haengematte", the welfare hammock, has received accolades in some quarters, but workers are the ones feeling pains. Ironically, many workers also blame technology for their woes, arguing that companies are using technology to improve productivity, and with automation, there is less need for workers. If this argument held absolutely, then, the companies would not have to shut plants, down. They would simply fill them up with robots, but they cannot do that because human beings are an integral part of computer systems. The point in fact is that many automakers, for example Renault, which revealed its new strategy on February 10, 2006, are trying to open up new plants to build new types of vehicles. It is just that they are opening up the plants where they would have to pay workers less wages and benefits, and where the working hours would be more flexible, among other factors. Rather than work against workers, therefore, technology, specifically, healthcare ICT, would in fact, make it less likely for companies to fire workers and move their plants abroad. The health system in Germany, for example, is also under severe pressure, due to rapidly increasing health costs7. The country is trying to reverse this trend by increasingly implementing healthcare ICT, the success of which efforts would undoubtedly help reduce the health spending. German companies pay about half of their workers health insurance premiums, which in the first half of the 1990s was on the average between 12% and 13% of a worker s gross earnings up to an income ceiling. There is little doubt that pressure of health care reform in the 1990s has redefined the interactions among the state, sickness funds, and healthcare providers in Germany, which some consider ushered a new era. Despite efforts to contain rising healthcare costs, some researchers worry that entrenched rules and practices are stalling the evolution of statutory health insurance (SHI), with reforms hardly allowed to venture too far from the status quos. Coverage of the SHI, the nucleus of the country's health system has not changed much, still at about 90%, the rest of the peoples insured mainly with private health insurance. Strict budgetary efforts coupled with shifting costs on private households primarily via benefit exclusions and increased co-payments continue. Furthermore, these reform measures have not adversely affected health outcomes such as the population's self-assessed health and life expectancy, which by the way underscores the fact that spending less on health does not necessarily worsen health and vice versa. In fact, a research study conducted by the OECD not long ago showed that "expensive" health systems do not necessarily increase life expectancy. The result compared life expectancies and cost in several countries namely, the US, which spent about 14% of the Gross National Product (GNP) on health care and had a life expectancy for men of 71.9 years, and for women 78.9 years. Germany spent about 10.4% of its GNP on healthcare and had a life expectancy of 73.3 years for men, and 79.8 years for women, whereas Japan, which spent only 7.3% of its GNP on health care, had a life expectancy of 77 years for men, and 83 years for women [9]. While cultural and other factors might have confounded the results, the study appears to suggest that a country could spend less money on healthcare and still achieve its stated objectives, which of course implies depending on what it does with the money. It also means that countries should indeed intensify efforts to curtail health spending and focus more on rational health spending based on a clear vision of healthcare provision for its peoples, and an appreciation of the various factors needed to consider in the process, including the pivotal role of healthcare ICT in assuring the delivery of qualitative yet cost-effective healthcare. The central role that healthcare ICT would increasingly play in health systems worldwide would go beyond cost containment. It would also foster competition. Indeed, reforms in Germany are foraying in this crucial direction, despite institutionalized tendencies. There is increasing competition between sickness funds and healthcare providers, backed, in the main, by technology, and with implications for incentive structures in both domains. Questions regarding SHI financing, specifically whether contributions should remain proportional to income or if there should be a radical shift towards flat-rate health premiums have taken center-stage, the answers to which would significantly influence companies' health spending, and the prospects or otherwise of future retrenchment of workers.

There is no doubt that it is in the interest of companies to provide insurance coverage for their workers, although adherents of the worker-demand based theory of compensating differentials argue that this is because workers want it, and would purchase it via wages less the insurance costs rather than receive extra money, and have to find and buy it themselves. Even if this were so, companies should therefore ensure that they provide their workers the best health services, by embracing the measures suggested by Leapfrog, for example. On the other hand, opponents of this erstwhile standard theory not only argue that it lacks empirical support, but that in fact, workers covered by employment-based health insurance plans earn more rather than less than their counterparts that do not have health benefits[10]. They adduce other reasons, for example, the benefits employers derive from offering their workers health insurance, hence that it may be more profitable for employers eventually to offer a compensation package comprising wages and health insurance than the former alone. The benefits employers might derive from offering their workers health insurance include a healthier, more productive and happier workforce, costs and tax benefits, recruiting and retaining forward-looking workers, reduced worker turn-over, and reduced compensation and absenteeism, among others. In any case, does it not make more sense for employers to provide health insurance to ensure that their workers have standard health insurance benefits, to prevent a situation where workers seek coverage on their own with resulting different levels of insurance protection, which even if they reflected the workers' choices, may fall short of their employers' requirements? Furthermore, could workers not end up without insurance and have to deal with prohibitive out-of-pocket healthcare bills or difficulties receiving required healthcare? Regardless of where one stands in the seemingly endless controversy over which really benefits from health insurance, both parties have essentially, the same concerns, namely the provision of qualitative, yet cost-effective, and affordable healthcare, which no doubt both also recognize that healthcare ICT would help achieve. Let us for a moment revisit the issue of CPOE. This technology could give physicians, medications options, including highlighting indications, contraindications, and drug interactions that could turn out to be life saving, but also prevent unnecessary illnesses and adverse reactions that could mean another length of hospital stay and treatment expenses. Regularly updated, it could provide doctors with newer, less expensive, and perhaps even more effective medications. Indeed, in the US, the Agency for health Research and Quality (AHRQ) is funding more than $139 million in grants and contracts in the country over 3 years to support planning, implementation, and evaluation of healthcare ICT, including CPOE. Pfizer Inc. launched Norvasc (Amlodighting) /Lipitor, -both the most prescribed worldwide for the respective conditions indicated, brand named, Caduet, in the US in 2004. This single pill provides dual therapy, helping to reduce blood pressure and cholesterol, making it unnecessary to use two different medications for these purposes, thus reducing costs. It is the first medication to treat these two conditions simultaneously. Health Canada has also approved Caduet for the prevention of cardiovascular events for examples stroke and heart attack, in patients suffering from hypertension, and with further risk factors for cardiovascular disease. High blood pressure and cholesterol are the main risk factors for heart disease, the single leading cause of death globally, with 60% of all cardiovascular events recorded in individuals with both conditions. According to Pfizer Inc., over two-thirds of North Americans that have high blood pressure have poorly controlled blood pressure, as is the case with over 80% of those with high cholesterol levels. The results of a large trial with 19, 342 patients with high blood pressure that evaluated the benefit of atorvastatin in reducing the risks of cardiovascular events in patients with high blood pressure who have average cholesterol levels confirmed the benefits to patients of treating both conditions. Patients with high blood pressure that had only normal or slightly high cholesterol who took the medication had fewer fatal coronary events. They also had fewer non-fatal heart attacks than patients did on placebo. The Lipitor element of this medication could help prevent cardiovascular disease in patients that do not have coronary heart disease, but have its risk factors for examples, cigarette smoking, being 55 years old or more, family history of heart disease, and low high-density lipoprotein (HDL) levels. Would knowledge and appropriate utilization of this medication not help reduce morbidity and mortality due to these conditions? How much could this save in human and material terms? Would these costs not far outweigh the implementation by healthcare providers of healthcare ICT such as the CPOE and technology-backed, evidence-based practices that would facilitate physicians' access to crucial information on such medications? What would companies therefore lose not encouraging, perhaps even insisting on purchasing health services from providers that have implemented such valuable technologies? A review published in the January 24 issue of the journal, Circulation, indicated that US spending on the diagnosis and treatment of heart diseases, poses "a challenge to the sustainability of Medicare," essentially, because while health spending on these conditions continues to increase, mortality from heart diseases has not changed in the last 15 years. This again underscores the point made earlier about increasing health spending not necessarily translating to better health outcomes. Indeed, two papers in the same issue of Circulation presented results of the tracking of heart diseases spending in Ontario and the US, which again showed more money spent but less positive results obtained. Take Ontario for example. Between 1992 and 2001, electrocardiographs (EKG) increased by 62%; stress tests by 38%, perfusion rates by 137%, and percutaneous coronary intervention procedures, by 180%. The province spent about $3 billion on cardiac care in 2001, roughly 14% of its $22 billion health budget, but the result was an insignificant fall in mortality from acute myocardial infarction (heart attack,) and indeed, a slow rise in hospitalizations for heart diseases. The situation is not much different in the US, which in fact, has thrice the catheterization rates, as does Canada. These findings highlight the need to review treatment options for these conditions, for example coronary artery bypass graft (CABG), which accounted for 42% of all cardiac care spending in Ontario in 2001. They also underscore the need to step up efforts at the primary prevention of these conditions, so that people do not have them in the first place. Healthcare ICT would be invaluable in such preventive efforts, and investments in these technologies do not have to be excruciating. Researchers at the London's Chelsea and Westminster Hospital recently conducted a study on text messaging, for six months, the results of Chlamydia test to patients cell phones. The study, published in the February 2006 issue of Sexually Transmitted Infection, found that this method sped up treatment time. The researchers sent out 932 text messages to patients, and found that the method reduced the average number of days before a patient received a diagnosis from 11 to 8 days. It also shortened the time it took to receive treatment, from 15 to 8.5 days. The approach also reduced the chances of missed results. Consider how much savings could accrue from this simple technology in terms of the prevention of complications, reducing illness duration, and possibly absenteeism, facilitation the return to health and engendering the feeling of well being with resultant positive psychological effects. All healthcare stakeholders need to keep exploring innovative use of the technologies around us, and not just of emerging or sophisticated and expensive technologies. It also necessary to keep evaluating these technologies, to be sure that continued investments in them make sense. Such evaluations would also reveal aspects of the use of new technologies that need refining. AHRQ mentioned earlier for instance not only funds healthcare ICT projects, it also studies how information technologies affect clinical workflow, and AHRQ-supported projects assess the benefits and identify any problems in using healthcare ICT. Furthermore, AHRQ is collaborating with an organization of leading employers and key health benefits purchasers such as the Leapfrog Group, to develop ways to evaluate the effectiveness of CPOE and electronic (e-) prescribing in reducing medical errors. AHRQ is supporting these efforts to encourage and enable ongoing evaluation of CPOE and other healthcare ICT under deliberation for integration into clinical settings to improve the quality of health care delivery. An example of the value of innovative ideas is the reduction in wait times for joint replacement accomplished by Alberta province in Canada, recently. The province started a pilot Hip and Knee Replacement Project eleven months ago, and is already getting results, wait times for joint replacement reduced from 47 weeks to 4 weeks. The project has also slashed the length of hospital stays from seven to four days, which would no doubt result in significant costs savings. The core idea of the project is a multidisciplinary assessment clinic, using standardized criteria, which streamlines the referral process and reduces the number of unwarranted procedures, and monitors patients until ready for surgery, with family practitioners referring all patients to the central clinic, with clearly extensive technological involvement for communicating and sharing patient information. Some quarrel with the idea of centralization as compromising freedom to choose healthcare providers, although officials noted that patients still have choice but may not be able to see the physician they prefer if they needed the first one available. There is no doubt that such creativity blossoms in an environment that promotes research activities. Also in Alberta, the British-based Economist, has described the Capital Health Region, headquartered in Edmonton, as "a model of excellence throughout North America," in essence in recognition of its innovative ways of delivering healthcare. The Health region is not only excelling in devising new models of care in the clinical domain, it also actively promotes research among its doctors and other healthcare professionals, via its Academic Alternate Relationship Plan (ARP), better known as Alternate funding plan (AFP) when the University of Toronto in 1990, and Queens University in 1994, first initiated such concepts. The ARP, stressing the relationship rather than the funding part this time, and the partnership between the University of Alberta, the Alberta Medical Association, and the Ministry of Health, is actually a provincial program, hence in place in other health regions. ARP places equal value on clinical, academic, and administrative activities, enabling a physician to develop the job description that best suits him or her, receive remuneration as specified in the contract, but also to receive incentives for excellence, and lose money for mediocrity. The achievement of expected and specified outcomes is through an accountability framework, with government funding tied to collective performance of all doctors in a group. Government is thus able to explore different healthcare delivery models because there is no constraint on doctors by such restrictive payment schemes as the fee-for-service (FSS.) ARP thus enables the development of novel models of healthcare, many healthcare ICT-based, such as the variety of services obtainable via tele-health, telephone and email consultations, ambulatory and community care, and the idea of interdisciplinary clinics. There is in fact indication that other provinces are about to follow in Alberta's tracks with regard this program. There are other examples of healthcare ICT-based innovative ideas in Alberta. The province recently launched the world's largest drug database, christened, the DrugBank, developed by University of Alberta researchers. This web-based search engine delivers instant medication information. By merely typing in the name of the drug in the search box, the program delivers a load of information on the drug including indications, contraindications, side effects, molecular structure, drug interactions, and dosing, among others to anyone, patients, doctors, pharmacists, or nurse. There is no doubt that this program would help in reducing the problems of information asymmetry, and that it is another crucial effort in the bid to provide everyone with the health information that they need, which would help in disease prevention, and health promotion, among other health benefits. These benefits would in turn translate into less health spending, an appreciation of which the recent unveiling by the New Brunswick Health Minister, Elvy Robichaud of the province's $2 million multiyear Wellness Strategy demonstrated. Focused mainly on children, the project has initiatives such as a healthy food grant for middle schools and physical activity promotion aimed as tackling the problem of childhood obesity, and the Baby Friendly Program. To emphasize the increasing focus on disease prevention, in the editorial of its January 31, 2006, issue, titled, "Legislating prevention," the Canadian Medical Association Journal argued for governments to go beyond health promotion efforts and indeed, "use their legislative muscle to bring about changes in risk factor exposures of the population". The editorial cited World health Organization (WHO) figures indicating that 35 million individuals worldwide would die from heart disease, stroke, cancer, and other

61

chronic diseases. It also noted that chronic diseases would constitute 72% of global burden of disease in adults 30 years and older. Preventive measures could stop people from developing many of the chronic non-infectious conditions in the first place, could delay their onset and minimize their complications, and reduce their economic burden. The key point the editorial made is that we should not restrict prevention to the individual level, but that government should implement policies "that create preconditions for health and attenuate risk factors for disease". It gave the examples of such moves for examples in Canada being mandatory food labeling, and in the UK, the proposed Children s Food Bill, which if enacted would curb the sale of non-nutritious foods to children, and their sale in schools. Indeed, there should be more efforts geared towards prevention at all levels, primary, secondary, and tertiary. With primary prevention, we would be able to prevent diseases occurring in the first place. Consider for example, what such a simple measure such as taking folic acid could do to prevent diseases. About eight million children worldwide are born with a serious genetic birth defect annually, with at least 3.3 million under-fives dying each year due to serious birth defects, and an estimated 3.2 million of those who survive at risk of becoming mentally and physically disabled for life, of course with significant implications for healthcare costs. Yet, we could reduce death and disability from genetic birth defects by up to 70% by simply giving pregnant women folic acid supplements to minimize the risk of spina bifida. Furthermore, hundreds of thousands more children are born with serious birth defects associated with exposure in the womb to alcohol, or infections such as rubella or syphilis, all of which are preventable. Think of how much agony in families, and how much resources, financial, and otherwise we could save every year by taking such a simple measure, which incidentally requires intensive campaigns well before the pregnancy even occurs, which deploying appropriate healthcare ICT would facilitate. Recent research evidence suggests that eating plenty of folic acid, which is found in oranges, lemons, and green vegetables, could reduce the risk of Alzheimer's disease by half. Researchers who monitored diets for over nine years, found that adults who ate the daily-recommended allowance (RDA) of folates (B vitamin nutrients) had a reduced risk of the disease, their research published in the premier issue in July, 2005 issue of Alzheimer's and Dementia: The Journal of the Alzheimer's Association 13. The researchers analyzed data on the diets of 579 non-demented elderly volunteers from the Baltimore Longitudinal Study of Aging to identify the relationship between dietary factors and Alzheimer's disease risk. Participants gave detailed diaries on their eating habits, including supplement intakes and calorie amounts for typical seven-day periods, and the researchers examined the amounts of nutrients including vitamins E, C, B6, B12, carotenoids, and folic acid in their diets. Fifty-seven of the original participants developed Alzheimer s disease; research evidence showing that those who consumed at least the recommended daily amount (RDA) of 400 micrograms of folic acid had a 55% reduced risk of developing the disease compared to those consuming lower amounts. Research has also shown that adults taking folic acid improved their performance on tests of memory, reaction time, and thinking speed, and that a diet rich in folic acid may help protect against heart attack and stroke, and as noted earlier, adequate intake of folic acid by pregnant women prevents birth defects affecting the brain and spinal cord. Folic acid helps reduce levels of homocysteine, an amino acid found in the blood, high levels of which previous research has associated with an increased risk of Alzheimer s disease. Other studies in the same issue of the journal touched on other important aspects of prevention, namely secondary and tertiary prevention, the former which essentially involves prompt diagnosis and treatment of diseases, an important area of focus known to improve outcomes for example in schizophrenia, the latter, preventing their sequelae. Both measures not only reduce morbidity, but also mortality, and significantly reducing health costs. A review article in the journal for example noted that such efforts at early identification and treatment of Alzheimer's disease and dementia, should include the timely and effective treatment of high blood pressure. With increasing life expectancy in many developed countries, the prevalence of dementia will likely continue to rise, with cost implications for healthcare provision, which makes the prevention of cognitive disorders and dementia a foremost public health challenge in these countries. The author noted that hypertension is a main risk factor for cerebrovascular diseases and has a high correlation with cognitive decline and dementia. The author also stressed that epidemiologic studies have not only found an inverse relationship between cognitive functions and blood pressure values measured 15 or 20 years previously, they have also shown that the use of blood pressure lowering drugs helps prevent cognitive decline. Timely and effective treatment of high blood pressure could therefore, also help prevent dementia of the vascular or Alzheimer's type. Tertiary prevention, the prevention of the complications of diseases as much as practicable, including in some cases effective rehabilitation is just as important, particularly with regard chronic diseases, again with the chances of easing the socio-economic burden of these conditions quite high implementing such preventive measures. Healthcare ICT would feature prominently in many prevention programs, regardless of the prevention level. It is doubtless that both individual-and population-oriented preventive measures would complement each other in yielding the desired health outcome, which is the significant reduction in the morbidity and mortality from diseases in general, and in particular, chronic non-infectious diseases that seem to be the bane of our contemporary world. In the UK, where obesity costs the country about £3.5bn annually and up to a million people are living with type 2 diabetes without knowing, there is much enthusiasm about the government's recent health MoT plan. The plan offers voluntary medical checkups that would promptly diagnosis latent diabetes, for example, and identify those at risk for the condition and others such as heart diseases. Some at-risk individuals would receive help with changing their lifestyles, including the offer of personal trainers. Part of the government's plans to shift the country's National Health Service (NHS) care from hospitals into the community, it is in keeping with the increasing shift in the health industry toward population health. The major role of healthcare ICT in these measures is ever clearer to all health stakeholders, which explains the substantial investments of many governments in these technologies. Cost issues would always mark any discussion on information technologies particular at a time that everyone is thinking about slashing costs. The question is whether these upfront investments would not yield worthwhile benefits even if only in the long term. Let us illustrate this point with CPOE implementation in Iowa. Researchers recently constructed a simulation model using estimates of initial and ongoing CPOE costs mapped onto all general hospitals in Iowa by bed quantity and current clinical information system (CIS) status[12]. They obtained CPOE cost estimates from a leading CPOE vendor, determined current CIS status via mail survey of Iowa hospitals, and used patient care revenue and operating cost data published by the Iowa Hospital Association to simulate the financial impact of CPOE adoption on hospitals. The objective of the exercise was to estimate the costs of implementing CPOE systems in hospitals in a rural state and to assess the financial implications of statewide CPOE deployment. The researchers found that CPOE implementation would considerably increase operating costs for rural and critical access hospitals if there were no major costs savings due to improved efficiency or patient safety. Hence, there would be need for third-party subsidies, or increases in hospital fees for CPOE implementation to be financially feasible in these settings. The results were quite different for urban and rural referral hospitals, the cost effect much less, but still significant, and which nonetheless, the modest benefits for example, patient care cost savings, or revenue enhancement would be enough to offset. This sort of analysis by governments and healthcare organizations would help in determining not only where to implement which particular healthcare ICT, but also whether there would be need for other measures such as some form of cost sharing with users. The improvements in health healthcare delivery that the various measures discussed above would bring, including improving the health of the individual, reducing the prevalence of diseases, and reducing healthcare costs, would on the aggregate ease the health benefits burden on companies and reduce the need for the sort of large-scale layoffs we currently see in the automotive industry. There needs to be consistency, however, in encouraging healthcare providers to implement healthcare ICT. To their credit, incentives for such adoption have been coming from both the public and the private sectors. We mentioned Leapfrog earlier on. The Group is a major force in promoting healthcare ICT diffusion. There are also notable efforts among health insurers and software and ICT vendors. Medicare is also doing its part. It is not only offering bonuses for hospitals and physicians that improve the quality of their services, it is also requiring hospitals to show evidence of that quality improvement effort in order to qualify for certain Medicare payments.

As previously noted, changes within the health industry itself are having far reaching consequences on how the various factors involved in workers health insurance and indeed, that of health insurance in general are playing out. Other major development in the health and indeed, the insurance industries concern increasing cost sharing and deductibles, measures aimed at modifying consumer attitudes and practices regarding health services utilization. The idea is that by making patients pay more of their health costs, it would curtail any tendency toward frivolous health service use. These measures would enable employers reduce their health benefits costs, and they could keep some of the savings in the health Savings Accounts (HSAS), that workers could later use to pay health expenses. They would need to pay for further health expenses on their own if they exhausted the HSAS funds, until they get to their deductibles, which would again reduce the chances of overuse of health services, with cost-cutting implications. The 2003-tax change, an aspect of the Medicare drug laws, buoyed HSAS, encouraging individuals to buy high deductible premiums, being able to open a tax-free account with its equivalent, so long as it is not less than $2100 per family, whose balance could accumulate over time. Experts predict a significant increase in HSAS with more employers offering them in their bid to curtail healthcare costs. People may indeed, be more discerning with cost-sharing measures, but some worry that many might just forgo healthcare because of cost or become anonymous in the healthcare market, which could raise healthcare costs in the long term. The present Bush administration's push for legal reform in the private health domain could help ease such concerns. The President's proposal in the recent State of the Union speech for legislation to cap payments for medical malpractice lawsuits is one example, which could reduce "defensive medicine" saving significant healthcare costs, for individuals and for government. Another is the government's interest in deregulating the health insurance market.

By so doing, the industry would be free of the yoke of state legislation that some consider even oppressive, as in some cases, it hikes the cost of a health insurance plan by almost 20%. Tax cuts, not for companies, but for individuals, thereby removing the skew toward employer-bought, low-deductible health insurance, and more openness on healthcare pricing by healthcare providers, are some of the consumer-driven measures the present US administration appears to favor. The underlying assumption of this approach is that the misuse of healthcare is the culprit in the country's healthcare inflation, and to solve the problem requires broadening the scope of HSAS and making all health spending tax deductible, barring removing tax subsidies for employer-based insurance. Some experts believe that the combination of tax and legal reforms could reduce the country's health spending by as much as $60 billion, to just about $9 billion annually, compared with $1,600 billion in 2002, estimates of the total amount of Medicare drug spending in 2006 alone, $69.9 billion. They also contend that it would reduce the number of uninsured Americans by up to 20 million. Others argue that the administration needs to look at the economic burden of chronic non-infectious diseases, at the core of which is a combination of lifestyle issues and increasing life expectancies, for its plans to work. This is because these problems guzzle most of the country's healthcare costs, and individuals that have these conditions spend much more than even the high deductibles on treating their health conditions every year. This again underscores the points made earlier in this paper on the need for a focus on prevention at the primary, secondary, and tertiary levels, and on population health, all of which the deployment of appropriate healthcare ICT could help achieve, cost-effectively. Some would also argue that other factors come in the way of rational choices in health services utilization, for example, that the opinions of friends and families, regarding a particular healthcare professional might sway people toward or away. True, but here again, rectifying information asymmetry would help people make rational choices if they had the facts readily available. This is why some people support the idea of making public not just the costs of care but also the credentials of healthcare providers, and whether or not they have any problems with their professional associations or with the law. People are less likely to rely on word-of mouth recommendations if they had these facts, say available on dedicated Internet portals run by healthcare providers, even governments. Individuals would also be able to find the right doctors or specialists as the case may be, in the nearest location via such portals, and with the shortage of doctors in many countries not likely solvable in a hurry, the use of such information portals is only prudent. The concern that those individuals that cannot bear much of the cost of their healthcare would lose out in the new dispensation also warrants consideration, as indeed, insurance premiums in other plans would likely rise due to higher risk pool, as the healthier and younger workers leave the customary insurance fold. This again stresses the need for disease prevention, particularly of the chronic diseases, which combined with poverty, essentially means exclusion from the health insurance arena, but which, prevented via aggressive health programs, would mean, decreasing health premiums, and inclusion in the health plan system. These outcomes may time to become palpable but the measures needed to achieve them are the real solutions to our seemingly intractable healthcare conundrum. In April 2004, Sir Liam Donaldson, England's chief medical officer (CMO) called on everyone to make exercise part of their daily routine, and to exercise at least moderately for a half hour, children, for sixty minutes, at least five times a week. Sir Donaldson noted that physical activity is key to reducing the risks of cancer, heart disease, and obesity, and that there was compelling scientific evidence to show that exercise can improve health. The CMO added, "People who are physically active reduce their risk of developing major chronic diseases, such as coronary heart disease, stroke, and type 2, diabetes by up to 50% and the risk of premature death by about 20% to 30%," and that preventing obesity would require at 45-60 minutes of exercises. According to the CMO, one does not have to do all the exercises in one go, but could split a 30-minute exercise plan into three 10-minutes bouts for example. Preventing many of the chronic diseases with just exercises could save significant healthcare costs. Indeed, a report for the British government published earlier that year, indicated that the NHS could save billions of pounds a year if it focused more on preventing illnesses rather than merely treating them. All healthcare stakeholders must be involved in these preventive efforts, including workers, in the interest of all.

References

1. Available at: http://seattlepi.nwsource.com/local/6420AP_Wal_Mart.html
Accessed on February 09, 2006

2. Longo, Daniel R., Hewett, John E., Ge, Bin, Schubert, Shari BA. The Long
Road to Patient Safety: A Status Report on Patient Safety Systems.
JAMA. 294 (22):2858-2865, December 14, 2005

3. R.S. Evans et al., "A Computer-Assisted Management Program for Antibiotics
and Other Anti-infective Agents", *New England Journal of Medicine* (22 January
1998): 232⁻238; and D. W. Bates et al., "Effect of Computerized Physician Order
Entry and a Team
Intervention on Prevention of Serious Medication Errors," *Journal of the
American Medical Association* (21 October 1998): 1311 ⁻1316.

4. Available at: California Senate Bill 1875, 28 September 2000,
www.leginfo.ca.gov/bilinfo.html
Accessed on February 10, 2006

5. Business Roundtable, "The Business Roundtable Launches Effort to Help
Reduce Medical Errors through Purchasing Power Clout," 15 November 2000,
www.brtable.org/press.cfm/464
Accessed on February 10, 2006

6. Available at:
http://lfpress.ca/newsstand/News/Local/2006/02/10/1436102.html
Accessed on February 11, 2006

7. Huber, Ellis. 1997. Das Gesundheitssystem neu denken! Das Geschäft der
Medizin und das soziale Gewissen der Heilkunst. *Blätter für deutsche und
internationale Politik* 42.7 (July):853--861.

8. Altenstetter C & Busse R. Health care reform in Germany: patchwork change within established governance structures. *J Health Polit Policy Law*. 2005 Feb-Apr; 30 (1-2): 121-42

9. Der Spiegel. 30 / 1998. *Logik des kalten Buffets*: 64 –75

10. Simon, K. 2001. Involuntary Job Change and Employer-Provided Health Insurance: Evidence of a Wage-Benefit Trade-off? Paper presented to the U.S. Department of Labor/PWBA Conference "Why Do Employers Do What They Do?" April 27, Washington, D.C.

11. Strong K, Mathers C, and Leeder S, et al. Preventing chronic diseases: How many lives can we save? *Lancet* 2005; 366: 1578-82.

12. Ohsfeldt RL, Ward MM, Schneider JE, Jaana M, Miller TR, Lei Y, & Wakefield DS. Implementation of hospital computerized physician order entry systems in a rural state: feasibility and financial impact. *J. Am Med Inform Assoc*. 2005 Jan-Feb; 12(1):20-7. Epub 2004 Oct 18

13. Corrada MM, Kawas CH, Hallfrisch J, Muller D, Brookmeyer R Reduced risk of Alzheimer's disease with high folate intake: The Baltimore Longitudinal Study of Aging
Alzheimer's and Dementia: the Journal of the Alzheimer's Association Vol.1 Issue 1. Pages 11-18

14. Hanon, Olivier, Forette, Francoise. Treatment of hypertension and prevention of dementia *Alzheimer's and Dementia: The Journal of the Alzheimer's Association* Vol.1 Issue 1. Pages 30-37

ICT & Women's Health

Friedman and Rosenman first coined the term, Type A behavior pattern

(TABP), in 1959[1]. TABP describes a variety of behaviors that include an exaggerated sense of time urgency, hyper-competitiveness, a drive to achieve, and hostility or aggressive tendencies. There is an association between TABP and coronary artery disease (CAD), and a number of stress related health problems. TABP occurs in males and females alike, and in both, positively influence academic performance, but has a negative effect on emotional well-being. The positive effects of TABP on academic performance, for example, are desirable, but certainly not its adverse effects of mental health, or its link with coronary heart disease, for which some researchers believe the mood instability, disinterest in exercise, appetite changes, and other manifestations of the emotional problems, create the risk factors. Should individuals with TABP then not be seeking ways to jettison its negative but keep its positive aspects? TABP has served as a model of the importance of psychosocial factors in the origin of heart diseases, particularly coronary artery disease (CAD.) However, it has also pointed at the significance of psychological factors in triggering CAD. In other words, psychosocial factors could put individuals at risk for atherosclerosis and CAD whether or not they have TABP. Considering that, these conditions are the world's number one cause of mortality, should we not be interested to understand better how they arise, including their psychological origins? Is this not the more so that we might be able to prevent these psychosocial risk factors, particularly in these days that we have sophisticated technologies at our disposal? What would be the effect on health spending understanding the causes of CAD and other heart diseases, and in fact of atherosclerosis, or the thickening of the walls of blood vessel by plaque that results in the partial or complete occlusion of their lumens, the pathology that underlies CAD? Atherosclerosis is a vascular disease that, once present means that it could affect blood vessels in other parts of the body such as the brain, the lungs, the kidneys, and the liver. Should our quest for knowledge of every aspect of this and associated conditions not be top priority, particularly as they contribute substantially to the increasing prevalence of the chronic non-infectious diseases swelling healthcare costs? Lifestyle factors such as smoking, overeating, and lack of exercise, no doubt play key roles in the causation of heart and other chronic diseases. The question is if there are underlying psychological and social factors that are important in the origins of those lifestyles, or that trigger the expression of an underlying diathesis. If this were indeed, so, could we therefore, prevent the lifestyles occurring in the first place? Should we not be undertaking an in-depth exploration of these factors in a determined effort to prevent chronic non-communicable diseases, which would certainly reduce health spending significantly, engender healthier societies, and ensure the continued prosperity of humankind? In a study aimed at examining the epidemiological evidence to determine if there is enough support for the hypothesis that mood disorders convey a risk factor in the pathogenesis of coronary artery disease (CAD), researchers reviewed the related research on Type A behavioral pattern (TABP) and other variables such as anger and hostility and their links to CAD. They then analyzed the findings to determine any clinical patterns or similarities between behaviors of Type A and those in mood disorders. The researchers found similar symptoms and behaviors among Type A, manic, cyclothymic and hyperthymic persons, and enough historical and simultaneous epidemiological evidence to support the idea that depressive symptoms and mood disorders are toxic risk factors for CAD, and although considered it premature ascribe causative links between them 2. Should we therefore not be taking measures to prevent depression, or be diagnosing and treating mood disorders more promptly and aggressively, considering what effects they may have on the sufferer's cardiac health? It is important though to note that depression is an umbrella word, and we need to characterize it in order to be clear in our approach to addressing it and its related problems. Depression could be a symptom, a syndrome, or a disorder. Depression as a symptom is the subjective experience of a low mood, or feeling down in the dumps, or sad, without any other significant accompanying symptom. Often transient, an argument with a co-worker, spouse, flunking a class test, or any relatively minor stressor could trigger this sort of depression, which some experts call demoralization. When other symptoms for example, poor or increased appetite, poor concentration and sleep, weight loss, or gain, guilt, loss of interest in what one used to enjoy, and loss of libido, are also present, we have a depressive syndrome or a disorder with the cause of syndrome known. Depression could also be a component of a variety of disorders, for example bipolar disorder, or secondary to a medical illness such as stroke. It could also be substance-induced, such as by alcohol or illicit drugs such as cocaine or triggered by prescription medications for example some anti-hypertensive drugs. Therefore, we need to base our efforts at preventing depression on a thorough understanding of these varieties of depression and mood disorders. It is clear from the above characterization that it is possible to prevent depression in many cases. Healthcare ICT can help significantly in this regard. Some researchers emphasize the role of possible dysfunctions in catecholamine and cortisol, hormones that play key roles in our flight/fight stress reaction, among other functions, in the underlying pathology of depression. Should we not engage in more research in this and other promising directions in order to further elucidate such links? Could such elucidation not create opportunities for better prevention and treatment efforts, which healthcare ICT could help facilitate? What are the likely implications of these developments for public, primary care, and mental health planning, resource allocation, and utilization? For example, typically, the diagnosis and presentation of CAD is different between men and women, diagnosed earlier in the former, usually in their fifties, the sixties, in the latter, with men usually presenting first with myocardial infarction (MI) or heart attack, and women, with angina or chest pain. These differences are significant, particularly for women, whose heart disease, physicians tend to miss, the resultant delay in diagnosis with prognostic and cost implications. Could there be underlying biochemical or genetic basis for these differences? Does the environment play a role? How could our understanding these differences further help in developing technology-backed options for needs determination and resource utilization? Could these measures not help reduce healthcare spending overall? The recent decision by the US government to create two new, closely related initiatives to speed up research on the causes of common diseases underscores the urgent need for such research efforts. The Department of Health and Human Services (HHS) announced on February 08, 2006, that one of the initiatives would boost funding at the National Institutes of Health (NIH) for a multi-institute effort to identify the genetic and environmental basis of common illnesses. The other would launch a public-private partnership between NIH, the Foundation for the National Institutes of Health (FNIH) and major pharmaceutical and biotechnology companies, especially Pfizer Global Research & Development of New London, Conn.; and Affymetrix Inc. of Santa Clara, Calif., to speed up genome linkage studies to find the genetic roots of a variety of illnesses. The genetic analysis component of the two initiatives will complement each other. According to HHS Secretary Mike Leavitt, President Bush's budget proposal for fiscal year (FY) 2007 includes $68 million for the Genes and Environment Initiative (GEI), a research effort at NIH to combine a type of genetic analysis and environmental technology development to understand the causes of common diseases; a $40 million increase over the $28 million NIH budgeted3. Upon Congress approval, this extra federal funding will start in FY 2007 and continue for a number of years, in the first year, $26 million will fund genetic analysis and $14 million, development of new tools to measure environmental exposures that affect health. Secretary Leavitt noted, "The discoveries made through these efforts will ultimately lead to profound advances in disease prevention and treatment." Few would quarrel with the Secretary's optimism. Even our reaction to stressors and the extent to which events happening around us demoralize us may have genetic underpinnings. The Human Genome Project and the International HapMap Project, for examples, both with significant healthcare ICT underlay, could help to speed up the discovery of the genetic causes of common diseases such as depression, diabetes, hypertension, and CAD, and even help explain the gender and other differences that research indicates in their prevalence, presentation, response to treatment, and outcome. GEI will also fund new technologies to measure environmental toxins, dietary intake and physical activity, and to determine a person's biological

75

response to those factors, using new tools of genomics, proteomics and metabolomics. To establish how the environment, diet, and physical activity contribute to illness, there would be substantial infusion of funds into emerging technologies, for example, small, wearable sensors that can measure environmental agents that have contact with the body and individual measures of activity, and on technologies that measure changes in human biology, observable in blood or urine samples. The new tests will provide the exactitude required to help find out how these factors influence the genetic risk of developing disease, with the aim of producing devices that are useful in population studies; that could accelerate data processing; and could improve accuracy, yet be cost-effective. With its $14 million yearly funding in GEI's environmental aspect, NIH plans to develop technologically-superior measures of dietary intake, accurate personalized measures of physical activity, and biological measures that spot earlier exposures to potential toxins such as metals and solvents, and will also evaluate disease indicators such as inflammation and oxidative stress, which research indicates environmental toxins influence. With the pace of advances in technologies ever increasing, experts believe that these goals are not only achievable, but also that we would be able to predict disease, develop more accurate and effective therapies, and, eventually, prevent diseases from occurring at all. The public-private partnership mentioned above called the Genetic Association Information Network (GAIN), exemplifies the intersectoral collaboration in tackling health and other issues that will likely blossom in the years ahead.

Recent findings that indicate that many women experience a different form of

heart disease, which is more difficult to detect have prompted researchers to call for improved treatment and prevention strategies. A study published in the February 07, 2006 issue of the Journal of the American College of Cardiology[4], for example, noted that as many as three million women in the U.S. might have a cardiovascular condition. The study is the latest incremental release of findings in the ongoing Women's Ischemia Syndrome Evaluation, the WISE study, which started in 1996 and tracked about 1,000 women with the aim of improving diagnosis and expanding understanding of heart disease in women. Also termed coronary microvascular syndrome, the condition, which puts women at greater risk of a heart attack often goes undiagnosed due to its symptoms not showing on an angiogram, further escalating the risk. An earlier study, conducted in the 1990s by Dutch researchers of over 4,000 individuals published in the European Heart Journals, found that more than 40% of heart attacks might go unrecognized by sufferers, a third of male heart attacks, and over half of female, typically not diagnosed. The scientists believe that women may be less likely to suspect an attack as their symptoms are often less typical, for example they may have shoulder rather than the usual chest pain that men have. Women may actually think that they are suffering from a severe flu, that is taking a long time to recover from, and women with an inferior-wall infarction may complain of stomach pain. Women may therefore, not consider it necessary to report these "flu" symptoms and doctors may also not be sure whether to consider heart disease in their differential diagnoses. Furthermore, women and their doctors have customarily been more concerned about breast and gynecological cancer, than heart disease. Incidentally, prior researches have shown that certain patients, particularly the elderly and those with diabetes, can suffer a heart attack not realizing it, factors that therefore doubly aggravate the risks of undetected heart problems in women. These studies underscore the need for women and their doctors to be aware of the symptoms associated with coronary microvascular syndrome. Indeed, we need to do more to raise awareness of the signs and symptoms of heart attack, and angina, knowing which and taking prompt action could save many lives. The results of such studies as those mentioned above should receive due publicity, facilitated by healthcare ICT, which offers opportunities for deploying a variety of technologies in such awareness campaigns. Regular electrocardiography (ECG) could help identify women with undiagnosed heart disease, and women who need treatment. Considering the magnitude of the problem in both sexes and the real chances of women with heart CAD going undiagnosed, what would software and health ICT vendors lose developing portable and wearable, consumer ECG devices that could give individuals some indications of whether or not they have CAD? Even if such devices could only send an alert signal that could prompt the individual to take a next step, for example, do nothing, rest, and call the GP later, or call the GP or visit the ER right away, could they not help save many lives? How much could such devices also save in morbidity terms and ultimately in health spending? Besides clinical testing, women also need to exercise, and to maintain a healthful diet and avoid or quit smoking, in order to reduce their risks of developing heart disease, the awareness of which again, intensive and appropriate technology-backed campaigns could help achieve. It is also necessary to raise awareness among doctors, particularly, GPs, and ER doctors, who are often the first-line physicians that women consult. Researchers are currently exploring different testing methods using magnetic resonance technology (MRI), found to predict cases in the WISE study. With 480,000 women dying yearly from heart disease, more women than men according to the American Heart Association, there is no gainsaying the need for urgent actions to prevent it[6, 7]. Hypertension also becomes a significant issue for women under certain circumstances, for example, for those on oral contraceptives, many of who have a small but demonstrable rise in systolic and diastolic blood pressure, often though within the normal range. There are also reports of high blood pressure being up to thrice commoner in women taking oral contraceptives, particularly in obese and older women, than in those not taking them [8]. This is a significant finding considering the possible complications of high blood pressure such as stroke, which if not fatal could result in life-long disability, compromising quality of life, and increasing health costs. Furthermore, cigarette smoking, particularly in women 35 years and older creates additional risk. Indeed, experts recommend that these women quit either smoking or the contraceptives. Healthcare ICT could help increase awareness of this important health information that could save the lives of many women. That there may be women out there who use contraceptives and smoke cigarettes is certainly conceivable, just as it is that many of these women may not know the health risks, serious adverse cardiovascular effects[9], that they face doing so, particularly smoking over 15 cigarettes a day. Should they not have the necessary information alerting them to this risk? Some of this information might be available in the drug information leaflet included in the pack of the contraceptive, but many people may not read those leaflets, whose fine-print format some complain pose reading difficulty? This is indicative of the likely information asymmetry on possible health issues relating to contraceptive use. Therefore, there needs to be other ways by which women receive this information. Should women not know for example that experts agree that those women that take oral contraceptives should stop if they developed high blood pressure, which returns to normal in most cases within a few months of so doing? With pregnancy rates, for sexually active fertile women not taking contraception almost 90% at 1year, one may have to wager between continuing to take oral contraceptives if hypertension developed and risking pregnancy if one stopped taking them, particularly regarding those women for whom alternative contraceptive methods are not feasible. If they decided to stick with their oral contraceptives, they might need to start taking anti-hypertensive medications. Some might say that the doctors prescribing these oral contraceptives should inform the women about all these issues. Fair enough, but do all physicians do, especially in these days of ever-decreasing consultation periods? Furthermore, do doctors prescribe all oral contraceptives? Certainly not, as women could purchase postcoital oral/emergency contraceptive pills (ECP), or the so-called "morning after pills" over the counter in some countries even in the developed world. Yet, many women may not know about the withdrawal from the market of some products with the original Yuzpe regimen because they are only about 75% effective, and have troublesome side effects such as nausea and vomiting. Even the newer progestin-only ECPs called Plan B in the US and Canada, Levonelle in the UK, and NorLevo in France, are having difficulties receiving FDA approval in the US. Barr Laboratories, for example, has been seeking FDA approval for nonprescription sales of its emergency contraceptive Plan B, for some time now with no success. FDA in May 2004 issued a "not approvable" letter to the company after its original application, citing inadequate data on its use among girls under age 16 years. The company submitted a revised application to make nonprescription Plan B available only to women ages 17 years and older, approval for which the former FDA Commissioner Lester Crawford in August 2005 announced that the agency would indefinitely defer. The agency then initiated a 60-day public comment period on it, which expired on Nov. 1, 2005. The agency received about 10,000 comments, which it is currently analyzing before it makes a final decision on the application. Some States, for example New Hampshire allow pharmacists but only those who participate in a voluntary training session the States' Board of Pharmacy sponsors to dispense ECPs without a prescription. The State's current law mandates that pharmacists dispense ECP to a woman regardless of age, as long as the woman has had unprotected sex in the last five days, has had her period in the last four weeks and has signed a consent form. However, there are new bills in the legislature that would restrict the current laws, for example, mandating parental consent for sale to minors. Massachusetts legislators are also debating whether to require parental consent in cases involving minors. Maryland lawmakers are currently considering a bill that would allow pharmacists to dispense non-prescribed ECPs to women, which could prevent pregnancy if taken up to 72 hours after intercourse. The bill stresses that licensed pharmacists and the Maryland Department of Health and Mental Hygiene would develop guidelines to determine who would be able to obtain ECPs and under what conditions, and that participating pharmacists would have to complete a training program and pay certain fees. There is no doubt about the importance of these issues in the body politic but are women aware of the various issues relating to ECPs and oral contraceptives in general, and how they affect their health? Many women on oral contraceptives, for instance, may not know that because vitamin C competes for active sulfate in the intestinal wall and makes ethinyl estradiol, the estrogen in some estrogen/progestin-type oral contraceptive, more bioavailable that the erratic use of vitamin C can cause breakthrough bleeding[10]. Many women may also not know that they could be twice as likely to develop blood clots taking some forms of birth control patch rather than oral contraceptives. The high inadvertent pregnancy rate in many countries is a major public health concern, which makes the correction of the asymmetry of health information on the use of oral contraceptives, which by no means is insignificant, imperative. The morbidities and mortalities associated with such use are many, and some, for example, that women who have hypertension, smoke, or have migraine headaches and use oral contraceptives have a higher risk of strokes[11], are potentially life threatening. Of course, besides preventing pregnancy, some oral contraceptives have other benefits such as increasing bone density, reducing the risk of ectopic pregnancy, improving dysmenorrheal from endometriosis, decreasing the risk of endometrial and ovarian cancer, and of menstrual blood loss and anemia. Some also stall hirsutism, improve acne, prevent atherogenesis, and improve rheumatoid arthritis. Again, women should know about these positive effects of some oral contraceptives. Existing and emerging multimedia technologies would facilitate the diffusion of these crucial facts about oral contraceptives, and indeed, all other important health issues pertaining to women. Some of these technologies are Internet-based, others enabled by advances in mobile and wireless technologies. There is a surfeit of health information on the Internet even now, but how much of that information is reaching women, or anyone else interested? How much of that information is current, and how often does the publisher update the information? Indeed, is not much of such information skewed to meet the publishers' marketing needs? Efforts must continue to provide current and relevant health information to its target audience. All healthcare stakeholders must engage in such efforts, which should exploit the opportunities that the relentless advance of healthcare ICT offers. Outpatient, community, children, and specialist clinics, ER waiting rooms, and those in physician practices are excellent avenues for disseminating vital health information. Health education posters adorned the walls of such places, mostly drawings and health statements, and no doubt helped pass on important health information targeted at attendees. Now that we have the opportunity, could we not replace those static messages with multimedia animated ones, tailored to specific patient populations and needs? A recent study in Quebec for example noted that antismoking health education campaigns that showed the pathological consequences of smoking such as rotten teeth on cigarette packs had negligible deterrent effects. The researchers suggested replacing those morbid messages with targeted ones would be more effective, for example, that to want to kiss with rotten, smelly teeth is anything but cool would resonate better with young people. Multimedia messages in healthcare settings could be in the form of cartoons shown on TVs in the clinics, or accessible on the Internet, and shown on computer screens or displayed across plain walls in the clinics, where the posters used to be for example. The URLs of the website where patients could find a video feed of the same and other messages displayed along would help disseminate the information to friends and relatives of the attendees, and enable the latter to view the messages again in their own time. They could view the programs on cell phones, on which individuals would also be able to view live TV programs, including health programs, soon. Offices, factories, schools, and even religious and other establishments could display health messages in ingenious ways best suited to their respective environments and audiences. Such messages would not only help prevent illnesses but would be morale boosters that could facilitate a sense of being an integral part of the establishment. Healthcare providers and professionals, for example, social workers, psychologists, home care and community nurses, could collaborate to show health campaign materials in their respective care locations, via appropriate Internet links, or e-health, health telematics or other digital health technologies.

Standardization and interoperability problems however, could hamper the

effective use of these technologies, even in a unitary healthcare delivery system, for example, a mainly publicly financed health system such as in Canada. These problems become even more prominent with healthcare providers, and others that use patient information having to communicate and share such information between disparate health systems. A woman's obstetrician might want her physician to know for example that she is now on oral contraceptives, just in case she forgets to inform her physician or her physician forgets to ask. Such information might alert the physician to changes in her physical health, for example, blood pressure that could signal the need to stop the oral contraceptive and to refer her back to her obstetrician for re-evaluation for other forms of contraception, moves that could save her life and prevent unwanted pregnancies, with likely positive consequence for her emotional wellbeing. However, even if both doctors had electronic medical records (EMR), it would still be impossible to communicate such information without their respective systems able to "speak" with each other. Canada Health Infoway is investing substantially into developing the infrastructure to enable such communication in the public health system across the country, but what would happen if there the private health sector in the country blossomed? How would information systems in the public and private health sectors communicate seamlessly? Would there be need to legislate standardization for both sectors, as for example with Article II of the US Health Insurance Portability and Accountability Act of 1996 (HIPAA)? The Act, in addition to addressing the security and privacy of health data, mandates the Department of Health and Human Services (HHS) to establish national standards for electronic health care transactions and national identifiers for providers, health plans, and employers. Would it not be necessary for some legislation to adopt standards in both the public and private health sectors to improve the efficiency and effectiveness of the country's health care system, in addition to promoting the pervasive utilization of electronic data interchange in health care and healthcare ICT diffusion in general? The Quebec government announced on February 16, 2006 that it is committed to a strong public health care system but that it would allow some private sector participation in healthcare delivery with individuals able to use private healthcare providers if they had to wait longer than six months for knee replacement, hip replacement, or cataract surgery. The public health system will still cater for life threatening situations for example heart surgery or cancer care. The policy shift is apparently sequel to a Supreme Court of Canada ruling in June 2005 that affirmed that ban by the province on private health care violated the rights of patients who were required to wait for treatment. The province's plan is for both systems to be complementary by ensuring that Quebecers will no longer have to wait longer than six months for the stated procedures. The government will if necessary, outsource treatment to private clinics if the wait list was three months longer than the guaranteed six-month waiting period. The government also plans to send patients out of the province or even out of the country, including to the U.S., for the necessary treatment, or patients can choose to use their own medical insurance to have the procedure done at a private clinic outside the public system, if wait times were longer than nine months. The government also plans to legislate wait times for cancer and heart surgeries, even as they remain the sole responsibility of the public health system. Some, for example Dr. Jacques Chaoulli, who originally took the case to the Supreme Court, do not consider the government's move adequate to protect the rights of patients, but others welcome it. Over a hundred doctors in Quebec have already opted out of the public system, patients paying as much as $12,000 in some practices for knee and hip replacement surgery. In his reaction to the Quebec government's announcement, the Federal Health Minister Tony Clement welcomed the province's decision to resort to privately delivered health care, although noted that the province will not receive additional federal funds to offset the costs of its planned care guarantee. The Minister indicated that the 10-year, $41-billion health agreement that the former Prime Minister Paul Martin signed with the provinces in 2004 already gave wait-times reduction programs more funds, and noted the likelihood that other provinces could adopt the Quebec model. According to the Minister, "There's a lot of creativity, we think, that can be encouraged within the Canada Health Act that will make our system more accessible." Mr. Clement also noted that he has no problems with the private-sector aspect of Quebec's plan, and that in fact, the federal government will encourage provinces to seek novel and innovative approaches to improve health delivery, even if it meant increased private sector involvement. The Minister however, made it clear that such approaches have to be within the context of a universally accessible health-care system and promote accessibility within that system. Other provinces such as British Columbia and Alberta are putting measures in place toward a mixture of private and public health care delivery, embodied in the principles of sustainability to the Canada Health Act, and the "Third Way", respectively of these two provinces. Private healthcare organizations are also emerging in different parts of the country. Would this development, if it became ubiquitous, not likely further highlight the need for healthcare ICT diffusion in the country, and the need for standardization and interoperability of health information systems? There is clearly a need for ongoing research efforts in this direction, as with those for example of researchers working on a prototype knowledge-sharing system that could enable individuals using disparate systems, and even from different professional areas share and communicate information better and collaborate more effectively. Projects such as the European Union's (EU) WIDE project12, aim to achieve this goal by offering different users a convenient and effective way to access shared information sources without having to adapt to a special terminology, using semantic Web-based rather than conventional information retrieval technologies, thus creating opportunities for innovative approaches to information retrieval, knowledge management, and online partnership. The use of metadata, semantic annotations of documents and ontologies, what terms and concepts in a domain mean and hierarchical associations, facilitates the interpretation of user queries and their automatic connection to the analogous information sources, the query result emanating from unlike information sources thereafter integrated on a semantic plane. The applications of this emerging single user interface, yet multi-user system, built initially for use in engineering processes by varied development teams, to facilitate online-shared efforts at creating process-oriented queries and the appraisal of their outcome would likely spread to other fields, including healthcare in the near future. Such optimism may sound utopian to some, but it perhaps says much for the desperation many now feel about the current fragmented state of health information systems, and its detrimental effect on patients, who do not receive the qualitative healthcare that they expect as a result, that we must seek help from whichever possible source it could come. This sense of urgency for a solution to the problem is evident in the recommendations of the Congress-established, Commission on Systemic Interoperability (CSI) in its October 2005 report titled "Ending the Documentation Game: Connecting and Transforming Your Healthcare through Information Technology"13. Besides its fourteen recommendations, the report gave real-life case scenarios of the benefits of interoperable healthcare ICT on our lives. Indeed, interoperability is at the very core of the raison d'etre for healthcare ICT, which is not just about a physician deploying healthcare ICT, but in being able to communicate and share data and information crucial to patient care as and when needed. In other words, what is the value of electronic health records, for example, if there were no information sharing? How could we be talking about healthcare ICT diffusion when we lack standards and interoperability? To be sure, there is already interoperability within the health system, albeit, via paper trails, and telephones, but these are the most rudimentary of the four interoperability levels that the US-based, Center for Information Technology Leadership, for example, recommends. The next level is data transmission via emails and faxes, the third, data that machine could organize, for example tagged documents and images, and fourth, maneuverable data, for example readable, interpretable, and automatically possible to integrate between say lab, radiology, or other systems and the EHR in disparate facilities. The need for standards for capture, storage, and communication, and for data and information integrity, security, privacy, and confidentiality becomes immediately obvious and critical, at this highest level of interoperability. What also becomes clear is the need for attitudinal changes for people to want to share information, anyway, which no amount of healthcare ICT diffusion could ensure, without the cooperation of the people in whose custody the information is, and who should be passing it on. In short, every country needs to adopt a tripartite approach, namely one that addresses the technical, business, and human issues involved in successful interoperability, and to achieve pervasive and interoperable healthcare ICT, including EHR, countries need to promote adoption of healthcare ICT, standards and interoperability, and develop the necessary infrastructure and networks to facilitate data and information communication and sharing. Simultaneously with each of these processes, countries also need to create institutional structures and to develop programs to encourage appropriate attitudinal changes among end-users of the technologies proposed and implemented. The US Office of the National Coordinator for Health Information Technology (ONCHIT) in November 2005 announced four contracts for developing a national health information framework, initiating the development of the four pillars of an interoperable health information-exchange network, under which contracts four collaborative efforts will develop models for a standards-based national data exchange network. This will establish the chances of national network interoperability, thus moving the current enterprise and regional networks forward, ONCHIT having awarded the contracts for the three other pillars in October 2005, namely, IT product certification, which will prescribe product functions and specifications to ensure interoperability; and data standards, which is specifying technical standards and data harmonization to facilitate data portability. The third pillar, privacy and security, is critical in itself and to assure consumer confidence, whose concern particularly as patient information moves from place to place, and across vast networks, will likely heighten. There is no doubt that these measures on completion will significantly improve healthcare delivery in the US. Imagine a woman that suddenly the falls and loses consciousness at a friend's place, and is rushed to the ER. The friend could not give much history and the woman, of course, being unconscious, could not. With technologies that enable patient data exchange in situ, it would be possible for the ER client services department not only to determine in which other hospital her medical records are, but also to access them. Such access at the point of care could be life saving, for example as it could reveal important past history of illness and medication history that could help with her treatment and improve the likely outcome of her condition. This example also shows the need for healthcare providers to adopt and implement healthcare ICT. Let us assume for instance that this incident occurred in a remote community, and she was rushed to the local community health center, the healthcare professional there, doctor, nurse, or physician, able to clinically diagnose her as having a stroke but has no training or experience in administering a tissue plasminogen activator, or blood clot dissolver, tPA. Indeed, many acute ischemic stroke patients at community hospitals do not receive tPA, the only FDA-approved medication for the treatment of acute stroke because the patient must receive the medication within 3 hours of symptom onset according to FDA guidelines. For many such centers or hospitals, which also often do not have ready access to neurologists, it might be too late for tPA treatment to transport the woman to a center where she could receive the treatment. Telemedicine could facilitate the provision of this timely therapy in such community settings. Two-way videoconferencing would enable stroke experts to see the patient and consult with doctors at these community health centers and hospitals. Implementing telemedicine technologies in such settings would make it possible for experts in stroke care to guide local ER doctors to conduct a neurological assessment, speedily review imaging, and discuss treatment options, for example tPA. Telemedicine-guided tPA therapy is not only possible, it makes such a life saving treatment that would otherwise be lacking, possible. With the morbidity and mortality from stroke quite high, along with other cardiovascular diseases the third leading cause of death in the US, experts recommend that community health centers and hospitals should either develop a stroke center or collaborate with medical centers that have stroke expertise, using telemedicine to steer stroke management. Indeed, government and private organizations are assisting in narrowing the gap between urban and rural healthcare, using telemedicine. The U.S. Department of Agriculture (USDA) Rural Utilities Service in September 2005, for example, awarded Doctors Telehealth Network almost $10 million in new funding. The Orange County, California-based company utilizes modern an d sophisticated teleconferencing and telemedicine technologies to provide healthcare to patients in remote locations. These technologies enable the transmission via a secure online network, of data and information from digital medical devices, such as electronic stethoscopes and electrocardiograms, to off-site providers, and video conferencing allows physicians and nurses to perform real-time medical examinations with patients in these remote settings. President Bush planned to spend over $100 million on telemedicine and other health-related information technology in 2005, the ONCHIT boss Dr. David Brailer has issued a challenge to all health plans to match or surpass federal funds for telehealth programs. With the increasing emphasis on community care, home teleheath could help in the efforts to manage illnesses at home, which many agree would improve the quality of life of the patient, who is able to receive excellent health services in the comfort of their homes and among their loved ones. It would also be convenient for the elderly and the disabled, and those that live on remote farms with restricted accessibility to health centers and hospitals. By reducing hospitalization stays, such domiciliary treatment would also help reduce healthcare costs substantially, particularly transportation costs from remote locations. Home telehealth involves the use of video conferencing or remote monitoring devices in patients' homes. Nurses, typically RNs, have customarily performed hardware installation of and training patients to use the Home Telemedicine Units (HTUs) blood pressure cuffs, and fingerstick glucose meters. There is likely to be increasing adoption of home telehealthcare in the years ahead. Telehealth use in Canada is quite extensive, particularly to provide accessible health services to peoples living in remote parts of the country, among other uses. The British Columbia Telehealth Program for example aims to support health professionals at secondary care facilities, for example regional and district hospitals in two application domains, namely children's and women's health (C&W) and emergency room and trauma care (ER-Trauma). Other applications include a focus on chronic conditions, the management of which visual information helps, and which involves established clinical teams undertaking regular scheduled visits or in sessions scheduled well in advance at local health centers and hospitals. Besides clinical applications of telehealth, administrative applications in support of telehealth implementation, for example via facilitation of management and provider education, are important for successful clinical application of telehealth, and other applications for example educational applications also confer significant benefits on these technologies that would make the capital investments on them worthwhile in the long term. Further evidence of the value of domiciliary care and of technologies such as telemedicine that support such health services comes from a recent National Institute of Health (NIH)-sponsored study of half a million couples that revealed that spouse's hospitalization for a serious illness increases the partner's risk of death. The study confirms the relatively common observation of a senior who "dies of a broken heart" not long after the partner's death. The new study, published in the February 16, 2006 issue of the New England Journal of Medicine14, further shows that the risk is greater with certain diagnoses, for examples, dementia, stroke, and hip fracture, and that the risk remains high for up to two years, the study also demonstrating the important link between social networks and health. The study also underscores the need for financial support for research efforts by both public and private organizations on this subject, and for health policy makers to keep abreast of the findings of these researches. The findings in this study for example should prompt further investigations into the underlying mechanisms of the stresses associated with these hospitalizations, the nature and severity of illnesses, and the workings of social networks in general and their effects on our health. The findings and further revelations by future studies should no doubt guide policy formulation on protecting individuals from the adverse health consequences of the disruption of their primary relationships, a situation of particular relevance to women who tend to outlive their spouses in most countries. Indeed, it should also assist in initiating or reviewing telemedicine policies, as these technologies could facilitate the domiciliary management of many of the chronic conditions that seniors have, preventing avoidable hospitalizations, saving enormous healthcare costs. The period of highest risk is within 30 days of a spouse's hospitalization or death, the researchers observed, which again should inform service planning including the provision of support services during this critical period, services that should be integral parts of the value proposition of healthcare providers in our times. Indeed, the increasingly discerning contemporary healthcare consumer would probably be looking for such extra value for their money. On the other hand, these and other innovative services would be differentiating healthcare providers and sharpening competitive edge, increasing clientele of those intent on remaining in business, perhaps weeding out those that are unwilling to embrace the emerging higher standards of care. Competition would stabilize pricing and reduce insurance premiums, and with more people, being and remaining healthy with improved quality of preventive and curative services, insurance companies would not have to worry about adverse selection, hence would be even more profitable. Employers would also pay out less health benefits, would have a healthier and more productive workforce, have less need to move their plants overseas, and to retrench workers en masse. With regard service provision, the study also shows that the mortality risk increased with age and, for women of a hospitalized husband, with poverty, and that the nature of the illness resulting in hospitalization also counts. Thus, among men with hospitalized wives, the wife's hospitalization with colon cancer has little or no effect on the husband's subsequent mortality, compared to that with heart disease, when the husband has a 12% higher risk of death than when the wife is healthy does. A wife hospitalized with a psychiatric disorder increases her husband's risk of death is 19% higher, and with dementia, 22% higher. The researchers observed similar effects in women with hospitalized husbands, and noted that the severity of the disease, particularly the extent of its interference with the patient's physical or mental ability, seems even more important than whether or not it is deadly. Thus, spouses would likely need even more support the more disabling the disease is, and the more it likely deprives the partner of emotional, economic, or other practical support, or imposes significant stress on the caregiver, which again are important issues warranting consideration in service planning and resource allocation and utilization efforts. Incidentally, telehealth, one of the technologies that could make hospitalization unnecessary is becoming the hotbed of another major policy issue, outsourcing, in particular, an application of telehealth, namely, teleradiology. In the US, hospitals are outsourcing the readings of patients' X-rays taken in the middle of the night, to radiologists in India and elsewhere, made possible by digitalization. This offshore interpretation of radiological studies points in the direction healthcare delivery is heading or does it? Advances in healthcare ICT, the quest to reduce healthcare spending, and the need to capitalize on time differences enabling often-overworked US radiologists to sleep at night, among others would likely increase this practice in the US and other countries, for example, Canada, where some believe that the scope of private healthcare is likely to increase over time. Furthermore, the success of teleradiology is likely to inspire the outsourcing of other health services such as the analysis of pathology specimens, ECGs, and colonoscopies, lesser-paid technicians taking samples and conducting the assay, and the pathologist, who may be in New Delhi, interpreting the results. However, it is not nirvana just yet for that pathologist, nor are we at the point when off-site intensivists monitor patients in hospital intensive care units (ICU) in the US in real-time via closed-circuit television in Johannesburg, although that is happening within the US itself and the outsourcing of such services abroad may ultimately come about.

Regardless, not only is corporate globalization contentious, issues of training, licensure and credentialing, and remuneration, with the foreign radiologists involved in the outsourcing arrangement required to have US board certification for examples, are crucial determinants of its future. There are indeed, concerns about quality and safety, which are legitimate, although the distinction between what some might term protectionism, and others, genuine concern for breaches of quality would likely continue to generate intense debate among adherents on either side of the outsourcing debacle. Significantly, the consumer is unlikely to be standing idly by, increasing sophistication of consumer expectations of care, at affordable prices in tandem with the tendency of the primary objective of the private enterprise being return on investment (ROI) likely to be among the final arbiters. Consider the results of a study to investigate how satisfied Swedish women are with their antenatal care, the study predicated on the importance of other aspects of care besides medical care during pregnancy, for example, psychosocial support. A national cohort of 2746 Swedish-speaking women completed a questionnaire in early pregnancy and at 2 months postpartum. Researchers collected the data in 1999-2000. They found that most participants were satisfied with their antenatal care, but 23% were dissatisfied with the emotional aspects and 18% with the medical aspects. The strongest predictors of dissatisfaction were the women's opinions that midwives had not been supportive and had not paid attention to their partners 'needs, the women likely dissatisfied if they thought that they did not have enough antenatal visits or had met three or more midwives during their antenatal visits. The researchers also found that those with low educational levels were more likely to be dissatisfied with both the medical and emotional aspects of antenatal care. They concluded that midwives working in antenatal care need to support pregnant women and their partners in a more professional and friendlier manner, ensuring that no more than two midwives are involved with the care, in order to increase client satisfaction. It is clear from this example, that outsourcing has limits, too, even within a country. This does not preclude market forces within, even outside, the country, still operating under such circumstances, as the woman has the choice to change where she receives her antenatal care. The issue of opening up the service

92

industry such as the healthcare industry is creating furor in Europe currently, with the EU pitched against labor unions that argue that opening their labor markets to foreign service providers, particularly those from Eastern Europe willing to provide services for much less pays, would lead to massive jobs losses for local service providers. Some would insist that regardless of the country, it seems that there are very few options than for service providers, including in the health industry, to prepare to provide high quality and affordable services in the prevailing dispensation.

High blood pressure is a major risk factor for all types of stroke, and controlling high blood pressure considerably reduces the risk of stroke. Men and women with normal blood pressure, defined by Joint National Committee on Prevention, Detection, and Treatment of High Blood Pressure (JNC 7) criteria, (< 120/80 mm Hg)[15,] have only half the lifetime risk of stroke compared with people with hypertension [16]. Calculated based on data from 4883 participants in the original Framingham Heart Study cohort who survived stroke-free to age 55 years, participants then followed at 2-year intervals for up to 40 years or until they had a first stroke, developed Alzheimer's disease, or died, the study is instructive regarding service planning. It revealed for example, that the risk of stroke rose with increasing baseline blood pressure in men, and women, that during the study period, 859 strokes occurred, 86% of which were ischemic, and that women aged 55 years, or older had a lifetime stroke risk of 21% compared with 17% in men of the same age. The risks were relatively unchanged until age 85 years. That women have a higher risk of developing high blood pressure than men from age 55 years, that high blood pressure doubles the risk of stroke, and that those that have "prehypertension "(JNC 7 category Bp 120-139/80-90 mm Hg,) apparently are not at higher risk of stroke, or myocardial infarction (MI), bring preventive policy issues squarely to the fore.[17.] The question of whether to encourage individuals to measure their blood pressures at home in particular has been quite controversial. A recent study that compared self-measurement with office measurement of blood pressure, found that office measurement using conventional sphygmomanometers remains key to the diagnosis and management of hypertension. However, the study also found that self-measurement and ambulatory monitoring are useful to confirm the diagnosis, and to detect white coat, or masked hypertension [18]. The increasing shift toward community care means that patient management will be occurring more at home or in ambulatory settings. Many more patients will be using healthcare ICT devices to measure their blood pressures, hence the need for these instruments to be more accurate and reliable. There is little doubt that detecting an imminent or masked high blood pressure saves the individual potential morbidity and healthcare costs, even possibly death, and health services and employers, healthcare costs, absenteeism due to ill health, and substantial healthcare costs that would have gone into treating the condition and its short-and long-term sequelae. With high blood pressure increasingly prevalent worldwide, about 30%, compared to the 20% previous estimate, all possible steps need taken to reduce its global health and economic burden. A recent review found that the prevalence of hypertension was lowest among rural Indian men, 3.4%, and highest among Polish women, 72.5%[19]. In developed countries, its prevalence is 20% to 50%, in the United States, 27.1% in men and 30.1% in women, with like rates in Canada, rates in Western Europe generally higher than in North America, and roughly thirty three percent of peoples in Latin America, and a tenth of Chinese peoples with high blood pressure. Thus, high blood is a major health issue for women, even more prevalent than in men after a certain age, hence the need for increased monitoring of their blood pressure. This increased prevalence combined with the tendency for doctors to miss the diagnosis of CAD in women puts them at even higher risks of cardiovascular events and disorders, and warrant urgent policy measures, and sound management protocols. With home telehealth, for example, individuals could not only measure their blood pressure at home and be sure that they are doing it correctly monitored by a nurse or their doctor via video-conferencing, they could text-message the results to their healthcare providers, or email, them. They could also upload them into their personal health records (PHR), which their doctor could access, and treatment or the next appropriate step discussed with the individual and action taken. Their physicians could communicate blood pressure changes to other healthcare providers for example, neurologists, and obstetrician/gynecologist if necessary via electronic medical records (EMR), a move that could improve the quality of healthcare delivery to the woman, if not even save her life. Consider that the woman is pregnant for example, and has hypertension, which may even be chronic hypertension, that is high blood pressure present and observable before pregnancy or diagnosed before the 20th week of gestation. Could such information sharing not reveal the historical antecedents and progression of the condition that could assist both doctors in developing the most effective care plan for the woman? Would such information sharing not be more efficient conducted electronically and perhaps in real time than via snail mail? Indeed, a three-state prototype for a national healthcare information network, built by Connecting for Health, a collaborative effort of over a hundred organizations, has successfully exchanged information between disparate networks in three states, the organization revealed in a release on February 08, 2006. The participating networks included Boston, Indianapolis, and Mendocino County, Calif. New York-based Markle Foundation managed the project, and Markle and the Robert Wood Johnson Foundation funded it. The tests used a specially developed Record Locator Service, which does not store any clinical data centrally but identifies the location of records wherever stored, rather than a single patient identifier. Participants in the three states utilized 20 million medical records to test thousands of exchanges, with real records given fictitious names and other identifying features to protect patient privacy. The tests showed a high 90 th percentile success rate for receiving the records requested, with not a single case of a doctor receiving inaccurate information. These remarkable results confirm that it is possible to build a decentralized network, signaling that the move from regional networks to a nationwide network could now proceed apace. Carol Diamond, MD, managing director of the Markle Foundation and chair of Connecting for Health has said that the collaborators would release in spring 2006, further details, standards, technical specifications, and codes used in developing the common framework that enabled the data exchange. A major revelation of this test is that data exchange could occur without a national identifier allaying the fears of critics concerned about privacy, security, and confidentiality of patient information, and paving the way for more individuals and healthcare providers and communities to embrace electronic health records, and other healthcare ICT. The objective of treatment for women with chronic hypertension in pregnancy is to diminish the short-term risks of increased blood pressure to the mother simultaneously not using treatment detrimental to the fetus' well-being. Would both doctors knowing the woman's drug history, including allergies, adverse drug effects, contraindications, drug interactions, and dosing, information obtainable in EMRs at the point of care, linked wireless to a mobile device such as pocket PC, or palm pilot, or via the ER or ward workstation not assist in using safe yet effective medications for treating her condition? With complications such as preeclampsia, a pregnancy-specific condition, increased blood pressure along with proteinuria, edema, or both and sometimes coagulation, renal and liver dysfunctions, even convulsions, progressing to eclampsia, posing serious threats the woman's life, there can be no overemphasizing the need for such technology-facilitated collaborative treatment efforts. This is more so as preeclampsia occurs chiefly during first pregnancies and after the 20th week of gestation, possibly superimposed on preexisting chronic hypertension. Still on EMRs facilitating joint treatment efforts, that a woman for example has hypertension is not a contraindication to postmenopausal estrogen replacement therapy (ERT.) A recent study showed that in most women, blood pressure does not increase appreciably with ERT whether or not they have high blood pressure. In fact, hormone replacement therapy is beneficial on their cardiovascular risk factor profiles[20]. Nonetheless, a few women may develop an increase in their blood pressure due to estrogen therapy. Should all women on ERT therefore not monitor their blood pressure more often after commencing such treatment? Would it not be more convenient for them to self-monitor electronically and transmit the results to their doctors via any of the means mentioned earlier?

Osteoporosis, a skeletal disorder that make bones brittle resulting in an increased risk of fractures, is relatively common in women, particularly as the protective effect of estrogens on bones lessens postmenopausal, and is a major cause of disability, loss of independence, compromised quality of life, and even death. ERT can ameliorate the effects on postmenopausal women of bone loss and other menopausal symptoms, but researches by the US-based Women's Health Initiative (WHI) reveal significant potential health risks linked with ERT. This is prompting many women to try naturally occurring compounds similar to estrogen, for example, those derived from soy, termed soy phytoestrogens, whose long-term efficacy and safety are, however, unknown, and are currently undergoing scientific inquiry. Many women also use calcium and vitamin D supplements. A recent major WHI trial published in the February 16 2006, issue of The New England Journal of Medicine, showed that the supplements in healthy postmenopausal women, a daily dose of 1000mg of calcium carbonate and 400 IUs of vitamin D3, provide minimal benefits in preserving bone mass. The study also found that they prevent hip fractures in some women groups, for example, seniors, and women who took the full-intended dose of combined supplements. The study also showed that they do not prevent other types of fractures or colorectal cancer, and that they may increase the risk of kidney stones. This study provides guidance for women on the risks and benefits of using calcium and vitamin D dietary supplements, in particular that women over 60 years old should use them although not expect them to help prevent colorectal cancer. Osteoporosis is partly responsible for an estimated 300,000 hip fractures in the U.S. annually, with 4 out of 10 women over 50 years having a hip, spine, or wrist fracture in their lifetime. With 10 million people in the U.S. estimated to have osteoporosis and 34 million more, low bone-mass, that predisposes them to bone fractures the problem calls for scrutiny, including the use of technology-based education campaigns on the latest research findings on preventing and treatment the condition. That Quebec in Canada included knee and hip replacement as priority areas, mentioned earlier, attests to the importance of osteoporosis as a major cause of increased wait times and a key health issue in the developed world, with an increasingly aging population. Still on the study, it confirmed that even healthy postmenopausal women would benefit from taking these supplements, which it revealed reduces bone loss and hip fractures for some groups of women, and because hip fractures are more serious than kidney stones, the public health benefit of the supplements outweighs the risks. However, healthy women whose diets meet recommended levels of calcium and vitamin D may not require supplements. Colorectal cancer is the third leading cause of cancer death and incidence for women in the United States. There is therefore an urgent need to find ways to prevent it. This study however did not support some previous studies and polyp prevention trials that revealed that calcium/vitamin D could prevent this condition, again important information women need to know that are currently pinning such prevention hopes on these supplements. Such information would not only give women taking the supplements realistic expectations of the benefits they could derive from them, it would also enable seek additional information on what else research studies indicate could help prevent colorectal cancer. It might also enable the woman seek and acquire all the necessary information regarding the condition, information that could be of immense significance for her, particularly if she had family history of colorectal cancer, an increased risk factor. To highlight the point about the need for targeting information, consider the results of some recent WHI trials. The significance of the use of healthcare ICT in disseminating health information might seem trivial, after all, some would argue, there is already a surfeit of information on health issues on the Internet. Besides the other problems with such information mentioned earlier, including inaccuracies, staleness, and bias, it is precisely because there is an information glut that we should device other means of presenting current, important and accurate information targeted at appropriate individuals and patient populations in real time, and in ways that it would reach its intended audience. With the likelihood of health information increasing even further and more rapidly, this is indeed, an urgent matter, and one that should stimulate research interests in developing novel and innovative technologies, even using current ones in new and effective ways. Heart disease in women for example is an important health issue as the preceding discussion clearly shows developments in medical knowledge on which women need to know about and as promptly as possible. Women have been unreported and poorly represented, even excluded in many past studies on heart diseases, but recent researches indicate that heart disease is a key and pressing health problem in women. Indeed, experts recommend that women that have cardiovascular disease take aspirin regularly barring any medical reason not to do so. A recent WHI study examined the presence of a link or otherwise between aspirin (ASA) use (325mg/d and 81mg/d) among post-menopausal women with cardiovascular disease and a reduction in all-cause mortality and adverse cardiovascular events. After following the women, 8928 of them, up for 6.5 years, the researchers found such an association, a 17% reduction in all-cause mortality, and a 25% lower death rate from cardiovascular causes, although neither dose reached statistical significance versus placebo in reducing myocardial infarction (MI) or stroke. In women that do not have cardiovascular disease, however, aspirin reduces the risk of total stroke by reducing the risk of ischemic stroke, according another study involving a meta-analysis of six studies that examined the effect of ASA use and dose on cerebrovascular disease, three of which had no female participant, with females constituting 47%-100% of the other three. The results of the study showed that men who took ASA had a 13% increase in the total risk of stroke, which was not significant, but a 67% increase in hemorrhagic stroke risk, which was, and no changes in ischemic stroke risk. On the other hand, for women that took ASA, there was a statistically significant reduction in stroke risk by 17%, and 24% reduction in the risk of ischemic stroke, although the researchers noted problems inherent in such studies, hence the need for caution interpreting them and for further studies. Another WHI dietary modification trial, an 8 year-follow-up study published in the February 8, 2006 issue of Journal of the American Medical Association, revealed no association between a fat-reduced diet and reduced risk for breast or colon cancer, heart disease, stroke, or cardiovascular disease (CVD). However, two editorials in the journal cautioned about the trial's limitations noting that the diet studied was inconsistent with current guidelines for a heart-healthy diet. Nonetheless, the findings call in to

99

question the long-held view that a low-fat dietary pattern could reduce a woman's risk of breast cancer, only now tested in a controlled intervention trial. The trial, whose primary goal was to determine the incidence of invasive breast cancer, occurred at 40 US clinical centers from 1993 to 2005, and involved 48,835 postmenopausal women, aged 50 to 79 years, without previous history of breast cancer, divided into intervention and comparison groups, dietary fat intake significantly lower in the former. The result essentially was that among postmenopausal women, a low-fat dietary pattern did not result in a statistically significant reduction in invasive breast cancer risk over an 8.1-year average follow-up period. The researchers noted though that with longer, and planned studies in the future, trends observed in the current study, although not significant indicated that, the reduced risk linked with a low-fat dietary pattern might produce a more significant relationship. Despite these findings, the specific constituent of dietary change responsible for the trends toward reduction in the risk of breast cancer remains unidentified, and warrants further research efforts, as do how much of it a woman needs to take, when she should start taking them, and for how long. Future research might also reveal which additional medications or other additional interventions if any that she needs to derive full benefits from the dietary regimen. Now, are the findings of these trials the sorts of information that women have to rummage through the Internet to find? Should such vital information not target women, its delivery to women assured? Do the varieties of multimedia technologies currently available not afford the creative endeavors that would make such targeted information possible? Is the need for such information dissemination not itself sufficient to stimulate such creativity? What could be the costs of not making such crucial health information widely available to women? There is no doubt that many women would look elsewhere for help in reducing the risks of breast cancers, and use ASA if not currently doing so. Could the decision of these women not lead to better health outcomes for them? How much would such improved health and possible reduced morbidity and mortality save in health costs? Indeed these questions bear significantly on not only women's health, but on some of the approaches to tackling the perennial health issues confronting many a developed country today. They highlight the need for targeted information and research, which healthcare ICT could enable and facilitate, as value proposition of healthcare providers, or as social and community health-promotion services of public and private organizations. For example, IBM has combined its Healthcare and Life Sciences units to create information-based medicine, which allows for technologies, such as proteomics and molecular imaging, to personalize health care services, including diagnostic tests and medications, for each patient. According to Nick Donofrio, the company's executive vice president for innovation and technology, "We're just as interested in society as we are in business, ·.we'll have a healthier society, and hopefully they'll buy a lot of things from us." He was commenting on the company's announcement on February 16, 2006 of a collaborative initiative with Scripps Research Institute, in a science-cum- computer technology effort to combat potential pandemic viruses. The eventual objective of the project, termed "Project Check-mate" whose hub will be in South Florida, is to create models of potential flu pandemics, chart their courses, and develop strategies to outfox mutations. The San Diego-based biotechnology firm, which is also working with IBM in California on a similar research project dedicated to finding new therapies to treat HIV, will conduct research into virus-pattern development. IBM will use its Blue Gene computer, the world's fastest supercomputer, to interpret and compute models and disseminate the data. The project, which Florida Governor, Jeb Bush, described as an economic boom for the state exemplifies the sort of ICT-backed, collaborative efforts even in healthcare research that the health system needs to facilitate disease prevention, an important aspect of the new health priority orientation, and to improve the quality of healthcare delivery, with all stakeholders benefiting ultimately thereof. The examples of diseases mentioned above are not exhaustive regarding women's health conditions, but serve to illustrate the importance of access to timely and accurate information in preventing diseases among women, and in promoting their health. Information transmission could of course be in a variety of ways, including by word of mouth. No one would dispute however, that no other means of communicating patient information between healthcare providers is more effective and efficient than electronically. The availability and accessibility of such information in a timely and accurate manner could make the difference between life and death under certain circumstances. It is therefore only insightful that the health industry embraces healthcare ICT. As previously noted, prevention is becoming increasingly prudent from both health quality and economics perspectives. With regard women s health, there is no doubt that prevention, which could be primary, secondary, or tertiary, could significantly reduce the burden of diseases, and curtail skyrocketing health care spending. Preventive interventions, for example screening tests, counseling, immunizations, and targeted chemoprophylactic regimens, could substantially reduce disease prevalence and healthcare costs. Primary prevention such as taking a flu shot could help prevent the condition occurring in the first place. Mammograms, and pap tests for examples could help with early diagnosis and prompt treatment, which are elements of secondary prevention, and long-term evaluation and treatment, including rehabilitation programs, are all elements of tertiary prevention that could help reduce the occurrence and severity of the complications of an illness. It indubitable the key role that healthcare ICT could play in making the achievement of these goals possible, and in sharing the results of these procedures with the healthcare professionals involved in a woman's care. Many women, particularly seniors, use several different medications on a long-term basis. Prescribing and dispensing errors are commoner the more medications a patient takes. Such errors could create potential life threatening problems for the woman. However, the use of a variety of healthcare ICT, for example, computerized physician order entry (CPOE), electronic medical records (EMR), and electronic health records (EHR), and bar coding, could prevent these errors. Women are also starting to embrace electronic personal health records (PHR), which they and others that they authorize could access, giving the owner control over her health information, including the prerogative to make them available to healthcare providers in order to facilitate service provision. The widespread use of these technologies will certainly improve healthcare delivery to women and collaborative efforts will help speed up this process. Thus, doctors in some parts of the US will soon have access to patient medication histories using data collected from community pharmacies participating in an e-prescribing project, and medication histories made available to patients, according to an announcement on February 13, 2006 by SureScripts, an e-prescribing network provider for about 50% of pharmacies currently. Starting April 1, 2006, the company will be testing a service in Rhode Island, Massachusetts, Nevada, Tennessee, New Jersey, and Florida to provide doctors transmitting prescriptions electronically a single view of a patient's medication history. The service will collate data from pharmacies that have important drug prescription information such as, dispensing and renewal instructions and date and allergies, this information combined with that from other sources, for example pharmacy benefit managers. SureScripts hopes to test the medication history service in at least 10 states by fall 2006. A 2005 survey of almost 3,000 physicians revealed that access to medication histories was one of doctors' key priorities. The company is not expecting the service to be a national system for medication history exchange, although hopes it would promote the interest of doctors in e-prescribing and prompt electronic medical records (EMR) vendors to upgrade doctor' current systems to facilitate electronic rather than fax transmission of prescriptions. The company is also in collaborating with hospital information systems vendors to integrate the medication histories into hospital data, and plans to certify personal health records applications to offer medication histories to consumers, via Medem's iHealthRecord. The company notes that the service would enable consumers and their providers to access crucial information, and facilitate automated patient reminders and education thereby enhancing medication compliance, hence contributing to improving overall healthcare delivery. Both firms plan to ensure the security of patient records before commencing the service, and to test methods to correctly authenticate and identify patients for matching with their medication histories. iHealthRecord already has almost 50,000 users, mostly through physician practice Web sites, since the service launched 8 months ago. Medem, which the American Medical Association and other medical societies co-found, is a physician-patient communications network. Although it charges doctors $25 per month for the iHealthRecord service, the medication history service will be gratis. There is no doubt regarding the importance of current, accurate, and comprehensive medication histories as a chief foundation of electronic medical records, as the example of problems with paper records showed in the wake of Hurricane Katrina. Indeed, the American Health Information Community is exploring options for a nationwide medication histories networks. To make the service even more comprehensive and valuable to other healthcare stakeholders, SureScripts also plans to make eligibility and formulary benefits services available to doctors. This would minimize follow-up phone calls from pharmacies and prescription benefit managers, saving costs for all. To underline the significance of healthcare ICT for the future of healthcare in the US, the federal government plans to increase funding for healthcare ICT initiatives in the fiscal year (FY) 2007 budget, requesting $169 million in funding for these initiatives, a $58 million hike over the request for 2005. The government allotted $116 million in the fiscal year (FY) 2007 budget to the Office of the National Coordinator for Health Information Technology, which received $61.7 million in the fiscal year (FY) 2006 budget; when the White House had requested $75 million. The increased funding for healthcare ICT at a period the budget reduced many healthcare spending programs, including $36 billion funds reduction to Medicare over the next five years, attests to the bi-partisan Congressional support for healthcare ICT. It also confirms its recognition, as a major component of the quest to improve the quality of healthcare, yet rein in health spending that seems to be spiraling out of control, which recognition is equally evident in many other developed countries.

References

1. Friedman & Rosenman. Association of a specific overt behavior pattern with increases in blood cholesterol, blood-clotting time, incidence of arcus senilis and clinical coronary artery disease. *JAMA*, 1959, 169:1286-96

2. Barrick CB. Sad, glad, or mad hearts? Epidemiological evidence for a causal relationship between mood disorders and coronary artery disease.[see comment]. [Review] [63 refs] [Journal Article. Review] *Journal of Affective Disorders*. 53(2):193-201, 1999 May.

3. Available at: http://www.nih.gov/news/pr/feb2006/nhgri-08.htm Accessed on February 14, 2006

4. D. Lucini, G. Di Fede, G. Parati, and M. Pagani. Impact of Chronic Psychosocial Stress on Autonomic Cardiovascular Regulation in Otherwise Healthy Subjects *Hypertension*, November 1, 2005; 46(5): 1201 - 1206.

5. Available at: http://news.bbc.co.uk/2/hi/health/4708616.stm Accessed on February 15, 2006

6. Gueyffier, F. Boutitie, J.P. Boissel, et al. Effect of antihypertensive drug treatment on cardiovascular outcomes in women and men: a meta-analysis of individual patient data from randomized, controlled trials *Ann Intern Med* 1997. 126: 761-767. M (PubMed)

7. National High Blood Pressure Education Program working group report on hypertension in the elderly. *Hypertension* 1994. 23: 275-285. Pr (PubMed)

8. Woods, J., Oral contraceptives, and hypertension *Hypertension* 1988. 11: (suppl II) II-11-II-15. Pr

9. AHFS drug information 2004. McEvoy GK, ed. Estrogen-progestin combinations. Bethesda, MD: *American Society of Health-System Pharmacists*; 2004: 2932-47

10. Kubba A, Guillebaud J: Combined oral contraceptives: Acceptability and effective use. *BMJ* 49:140, 1993

11. Schwartz SM, Petitti DB, Siscovick DS, et al: Stroke and use of low-dose oral contraceptives in young women. A pooled analysis of two US studies. *Stroke* 29:2277, 1998

12. Available at: http://www.aramis-research.ch/d/17192.html#top Accessed on February 17, 2006

13. Commission on Systemic Interoperability (CSI). "Ending the Document Game: Connecting and Transforming Your Healthcare through Information Technology." October 2005.

14. NA Christakis et al. Mortality After Hospitalization of a Spouse. New *England Journal of Medicine*; vol. 354, issue 7, 719-730 (2006).

15. Chobanian AV, Bakris GL, Black HR, et al. Seventh Report of the Joint National Committee on Prevention, Detection, Evaluation, and Treatment of High Blood Pressure. *Hypertension*. 2003; 42:1206-1252.

16. Seshadri S, Beiser A, Wolf PA. Lifetime risk of stroke: results from the Framingham Study. Program and abstracts from the 29th International Stroke Conference; February 5-7, 2004; San Diego, California.

17. Mohammad Y, Qureshi AI, Suri MFK, et al. Is pre-hypertension a risk factor for stroke and myocardial infarction? Program and abstracts from the 29th International Stroke Conference; February 5-7, 2004; San Diego, California.

18. Staessen JA, Den Hond E, Fagard R, et al, for the Treatment of Hypertension Based on Home or Office Blood Pressure (THOP) Trial Investigators. Antihypertensive treatment based on blood pressure measurement at home or in the physician's office: a randomized controlled trial. *JAMA*. 2004; 291:955-964.

19. Kearney PM, Whelton M, Reynolds K, et al. Worldwide prevalence of hypertension: a systematic review. J *Hypertens*. 2004; 22:11-19.

20. Effects of estrogen or estrogen/progestin regimens on heart disease risk factors in postmenopausal women: the Postmenopausal Estrogen/Progestin Interventions (PEPI) Trial *JAMA* 1995. 273: 199-208.

ICT & the Health of Children & Adolescents

That certain malevolent characters prey on children on the Internet is well known. Such predatory activities harm children's mental, sometimes even physical health. A variety of software exists that enable parents to monitor their children's Internet activities, and efforts continue to improve the capabilities of these software. Microsoft, for example, is currently seeking testers to try an early version of new parental control software for Windows XP called Windows Live Family Safety Settings. Parental controls software allows parents to filter online content, in order to keep Web content that they consider unsuitable or inappropriate from reaching their children, for examples, pornography, gambling, alcohol, illicit drugs, and tobacco. Parents would be able to create individual accounts for children with Microsoft's new product. The software will also enable them to view activity reports on the Web sites that their children visited, and to disable the service when the parents themselves are surfing the World Wide Web. Microsoft is also incorporating parental controls into Windows Vista, the next version of its operating system (OS) due on the market by the end of 2006. Still on parental control, parents in Houston, Texas, may soon have more control over what their children eat by being able to track their eating habits via computer and to block some foods from the menu. All they need to do is sign up to a prepaid account that would enable them to log on to an automated cafeteria, and be able to know their children's choice of foods, and to modify them, if necessary. Subscribed parents for example would be able to decide how many burgers to permit their children a week, ideally in consultation with the children. Such services would doubtless, help parents, concerned about what their children are eating, when not at home, for example at school, or about weight and health issues regarding their children, keep track of their children's diets. This could help reduce the prevalence of childhood obesity, which public health data confirm has reached epidemic proportions in many developed countries1. In the US, the prevalence of overweight among children aged 6 to 11 years has more than doubled in the past two decades, according to the Centers for Disease Control (CDC), from 7% in 1980 to 16% in 2002, the rate for adolescents aged 12 to 19 years more than tripled, from 5% to 16%. Overweight, reflects less calories expended than consumed. An estimated 61% of overweight young people have at least one further risk factor for heart disease; for example, high cholesterol or high blood pressure, and overweight children are at higher risk for bone and joint problems, and sleep apnea. They are also at increased risk for social and psychological problems, for examples, low self-esteem, and stigma. Overweight young people also have more chances to grow into overweight or obese adults, hence at increased risk for weight-related adult diseases such as heart disease, type-2 diabetes, stroke, a variety of cancer, and osteoarthritis than children of normal weight do. It is therefore important to encourage young people to avoid becoming overweight and to embrace healthy lifestyles, including healthy eating and exercise. Research studies indicate that the prevalence of obesity in children and adolescents is still increasing, hence the urgent need for preventive measures of this condition. However, it is important to know the risk factors for obesity in order to deploy resources appropriately, and efficiently, critical to achieving this goal. Researchers have shown, for example, that prevention strategies focused on late childhood and adolescence, are in the main, unsuccessful, and that early life environment can determine later risk of obesity. A UK prospective cohort study to identify risk factors in early life, up to three years of age, for obesity in children in the country[2], after controlling for maternal education, which is significantly correlated with the development of obesity in children, concluded that eight of twenty five putative factors in early life increase the risks of childhood obesity. The factors include parental obesity; very early (by 43 months) body mass index, or adiposity rebound; over eight hours spent watching TV per week at age 3 years; and catch-up growth. Others are weight gain in first year; birth weight; short (less than 10.5 hours) sleep duration at age 3 years, and standard deviation score for weight at age eight months (3.13, 1.43, to 6.85) and 18 months (2.65, 1.25 to 5.59). Experts agree that identifying risk factors for childhood obesity is crucial to preventing it[3] and its associated health problems some of which are not only life threatening but constitute a significant

109

health burden. The authors of the study acknowledged that they were unable to analyze several other potential risk factors, for example physical activity and energy expenditure, parental control over feeding in childhood4, and gestational diabetes. It is important in order to develop effective preventive programs to research and understand how genetics and environmental factors interact in the etiology of childhood obesity, by no means an easy task considering that parents provide both genes and environment for children. Consider the issue of parental control for example. Children learn a lot about food and eating as they transition from the mainly milk diet of infancy to the complex diet of early childhood. Even this learning process has genetic underlay, including the unlearned preference for and rejection of certain flavors of food. Research studies not only indicate individual differences in the self-regulation of energy intake as early as the preschool period, but also a link with differences in child-feeding practices and children' adiposity. In other words, child-feeding practices could affect a child's energy balance through changing intake patterns. Indeed, there is evidence suggesting that imposing rigid parental controls could result in a child preferring high-fat, energy-dense foods, limit his/her reception of an assortment of foods, and disrupt his/her energy intake regulation by interfering with the reaction to internal hunger and satiety cues. Do these findings not have implications for preventive interventions? Do parents not need to know that regardless of their good intentions, their actions at these early stages of their child's development could be crucial to his/her energy regulation, which in turn could influence the child's weight? These studies imply the need for parents to be flexible regarding their child-feeding practices, including providing children with opportunities for self-control. Would it not be important for parents to know these facts regarding their toddlers? Healthcare ICT could certainly help disseminate such targeted information. The health industry is one of the most information-intensive, akin to the banking and financial service industries. It is difficult to access vital information and on time with the amount and rate of health information flow. This is one reason why the use of multimedia healthcare ICT is important in getting information to those that need it as soon as possible, as it may be too late to make a difference to the lives of many people otherwise. Furthermore, there is research evidence to suggest that individuals could increase their capacity to remember important information by simply filtering out the irrelevant information, giving some credence to the value of targeted information. University of Oregon scientists in a paper published in the journal, Nature in November 2005, showed that awareness, or visual working memory, depends on being able to discount irrelevancies rather than on the brain's storage capacity, that it is all about a neural mechanism much like a "bouncer" that determines what information reaches awareness. What we can remember then, according to this research is not how much we managed to cram into our brains as previous theories held. Consider another potential risk factor for childhood obesity. Research studies have revealed an association between exposure to diabetes in the womb and diabetes and obesity in the offspring, albeit confounded by genetic factors. However, studies have shown the risk of diabetes to be significantly higher in siblings born after the mother developed diabetes than in those born before the mother's diagnosis of diabetes. These studies concluded that intrauterine exposure to diabetes per se puts the offspring at a high risk for developing diabetes and obesity in excess of that attributable to genetic factors alone. To underscore the significance of the subject of childhood obesity, former US President Bill Clinton is collaborating with the Robert Wood Foundation on a new health campaign, which aims to improve the health of school-aged children by promoting healthier food and more exercise. The campaign is a component of the year-old Alliance for a Healthier Generation campaign, a joint endeavor by Clinton's foundation and the American Heart Association. Obesity rates in children ages six to 19 have tripled in the US in the past 40 years, and continue to rise, increasing the risks of type 2 diabetes, and other health problems, many chronic, with implications for healthcare costs. The pilot phase of the campaign, which starts in fall 2006, will give 285 schools in 13 states the resources to improve the nutritional value of cafeteria food and vending machine products, increase physical activity among students, provide health education and promote staff wellness. There is no doubt that there will be heavy healthcare ICT input in many of these programs, which will spread over time nationwide. A BBC News documentary on February 21, 2006 highlighted the abandonment of infants born to HIV-positive women in Russia, about 20 infants daily. Russia has one of the fastest-growing HIV/AIDS epidemics in the world. The state ends up caring for about two of every 20 children their mothers abandoned, many in state-run infectious diseases hospitals for at least 18 months, the period doctors in the country require to determine a child's HIV status officially. Stigma is at the core of these mothers abandoning their children. Many Russian women also do not know about the availability of antiretroviral drugs to prevent mother-to-child HIV transmission of HIV that they could receive in Russia. Abandoned children remain in hospitals indefinitely because orphanages often refuse to accept them, and those that do isolate these children from the other children, again because of stigma. What are the likely short-and long-term consequences of these discriminatory treatments on the mental status of these children? They are unlikely to be positive, most would imagine. Is it impossible to prevent such adverse effects? Certainly not, and doing so creates opportunities for exploiting the benefits of healthcare ICT in enabling large-scale health education and public relations campaigns, which could help remove the stigma surrounding HIV/AIDS in Russia, and indeed, elsewhere in the world, in addition to offering the affected children the chance of an improved quality of life. Let us illustrate the latter point with the findings of recent studies published in the Proceedings of the national Academy of Sciences, USA, in November and December 2005[6, 7], which attempted to extend the findings in previous studies that have shown an association between the neuropeptides, vasopressin and oxytocin, and social bonding in nonhuman species, to human children [8]. The researchers measured urine neuropeptides before and after social experiments in the children's homes, an accurate reflection of brain neuropeptide activity because the brain produces almost all of these substances. They studied eighteen adopted children living in orphanages in neglected, and twenty-one of similar age living in normal environments. The researchers collected urine samples from these children before and about twenty minutes after the latter had physical interactions with an unfamiliar person, and with the adoptive or biological mother, guided by a computerized "game". The mean age of the orphanage-raised children was 54 months, mean orphanage stay, 16.6 months, and mean stay in adoptive homes,

34.6 months. Vasopressin levels were not only lower for the orphanage-raised children at baseline, but also unlike for the controls, when it increased, did not change after the interactions with mothers. Although there were overlaps in neuropeptide levels between the adopted and biologically raised groups, there were no group differences in oxytocin levels after testing with unfamiliar adults and no significant changes in vasopressin levels in either group or after either experiment. The study is a pointer for further research on the subject. In particular, it suggests the need for a more in-depth understanding of the emotional health of orphaned and adopted children, the dynamic interactions of genetic and environmental factors on their health, and the possible implications of such knowledge for intervention measures and for the future of for these children. It is the more important to study these phenomena with the scourge of HIV/AIDS is leaving so many children behind, abandoned in orphanages and in many case under less than ideal conditions, worldwide. Canada plans to donate about $40.5 million to the United Nation Children's Fund (UNICEF), to help improve child health and survival initiatives, mainly in Africa, including about $7.8 million to purchase 1.2 million long-lasting insecticide-treated nets to protect families in Ethiopia against malaria. Provided through the Canadian International Development Agency (CIDA), the money will fund measles, pneumonia and diarrhea, and the increasing gap in immunization and health and nutrition programs between countries. A recent UNICEF Canada report released simultaneously with the announcement of the funding noted that despite significant progress made in reducing childhood deaths over the last 50 years, 29,000 children under age five die daily from preventable diseases, including HIV/AIDS. According to the report, HIV/AIDS is a major threat to child health, that mortality rates in 14 countries, nine in sub-Saharan Africa, is on the increase in recent years, chiefly because of the HIV/AIDS pandemic, and that HIV infects about 1,800 children daily, mostly through mother-to-child transmission. The report added that although there are effective treatments to prevent vertical HIV transmission, only 10% of pregnant women in developing countries have access to such treatments, and that HIV makes children more vulnerable to other diseases, for example measles, pneumonia, malaria and diarrhea. According to

Nigel Fisher, UNICEF Canada CEO, "With the advances of the past five decades, we could bring these diseases to their knees and break the back of the HIV/AIDS pandemic, but we need greater political will and action." He also emphasized the need to make integrated treatment and prevention programs available to all children to curb the pandemic. Indeed, all the political will without the appropriate action will still hardly yield the desired results. Thus, it is important to deploy scarce resources in the most cost-effective manner in order to prevent mothers, and indeed, individuals in general, acquiring the disease in the first place, and its vertical transmission from mother to child. Even in developing countries, with limited infrastructure, healthcare ICT could be critical in achieving this objective, deployed in tune with their available albeit limited telecommunications and other infrastructures. Again, though, even the use of these technologies, in addition to which considering the nature and extent of available infrastructures is crucial to its planning, needs targeting, based not on assumptions, but on sound evidence of high-risk populations. Part of targeting the information not only involving developing the most effective content, but also taking decisions on which of the available multimedia and Internet portals would deliver the messages to the target population most effectively. The need to capitalize on the benefits of healthcare ICT in delivering more effective, targeted health campaigns underscores that of promoting ICT diffusion in these countries as well. Many believe, for example that the global response to children affected by HIV and AIDS is not enough to match the enormity of their rapidly expanding plight, the disease expected to orphan an estimated 18 million children in sub-Saharan Africa alone by 2010. What are the likely consequences of this devastation on the children and the economies of these countries? Children living with ailing and dying parents remain particularly vulnerable, an estimated 4 million infected children lacking access to appropriate treatments. Could the proper deployment of technologies not avert such crises? Could the delivery of targeted information with these technologies with full consideration of the complexity and peculiarities of the social milieu of the targeted population, for examples poverty, distrust, and a lack of personal intimacy, all factors that could influence behavior change, not help prevent the disease in the first place? The

2006 Global Partners Forum, which the UNICEF and the UK Department for International Development (DFID), are hosting will bring together high level representatives from 90 international organizations, NGOs and governments in an effort to determine effective practical solutions to the plight of millions of children caught in the AIDS pandemic. The Forum, formed in 2003, aims to give impetus to meeting global commitments for children affected by HIV and AIDS, laid out in the United Nations General Assembly 2001 Declaration of Commitments on HIV/AIDS and the Millennium Development Goals. According to the UNICEF Executive Director, Ann M. Veneman "Children are missing from the world's response to the global AIDS pandemic, less than 10 per cent of the children who have been orphaned or made vulnerable by AIDS receive public support or services." The forum's foci include increasing access of education and to guarantee universal access to HIV prevention, treatment and care, the achievement of both of which healthcare ICT could certainly facilitate. There is no doubt that existing programs have left children and youngsters behind, groups whose knowledge of protecting themselves from the HIV virus, is crucial to breaking the vicious cycle of the infection. In particularly, ensuring that girls get equal access to education is also critical, particularly in many developing countries where they do not, which is perhaps why it is not surprising that girls disproportionately have HIV/AIDS. Here again, disseminating the appropriate information to the right people is no doubt an important component of any efforts to change attitudes to educating female children, and even in developing countries, multimedia technologies could help deliver these messages cost-effectively. These messages could reach many people via for examples, football stadiums, cinema theaters, mass transit systems for examples buses and trains, town halls, schools, hospitals and health centers, civic centers, workplaces, and portable radios, among others.

E stimates of childhood depression vary in different populations and age-groups but not only is it established that children suffer from this condition, adult diagnostic criteria apply in determining its presence or otherwise in a child. In Canada, for example, the estimated prevalence of depression in children and adolescents are 2% and 6% respectively, and depression causes significant morbidities and mortalities in children. Considering that children even as young as five years old could have suicidal thoughts, is it not important for parents to know not just how this condition manifests but also what to do, where to get help, and even to know about the different treatment options available to their children? As trivial as this issue might sound to some, providing parents with such knowledge could save many lives, and many families profound misery. The treatment of childhood depression for example has been the subject of media scrutiny in recent times, particularly with some studies suggesting that some of the most commonly used pharmacological agents to treat depression, the selective serotonin reuptake inhibitors (SSRIs) could trigger suicidal ideation in children using them. However, it is not clear that more recent studies that showed not just their effectiveness in treating depression and that remission rates with them are low but also that suicide rates actually declined with these treatments received equal media attention. This again underlines the need for targeted information, which healthcare ICT could help accomplish. Parents should know for example that Fluoxetine is the only medication approved in the US for treating childhood depression, and presently the only one with more than one positive clinical trial supporting its use. Parents also need to know that there is demonstration of the effectiveness in treating childhood and adolescent depression of non-SSRI medications such as venlafaxine, nefazodone, and mirtazapine, and that combination therapy, for example with an SSRI and cognitive behavioral therapy (CBT) is more effective than SSRI or CBT alone to treat depression. The Treatment for Adolescents with Depression Study (TADS), confirms that using cognitive behavioral therapy (CBT), a form of psychotherapy that focuses on managing negative emotions and thoughts, and fluoxetine (Prozac) results in successful treatment of moderate to severe adolescent depressions. Healthcare ICT could play a role in either the medications or CBT aspect of the child's treatment. Computerized Physician order entry (CPOE), for example, could help ensure safer medication prescribing, including providing the doctor important information on dosages, side effects, and drug interactions. Weight gain could be a major issue with some SSRI s, for example, a problem that could reduce compliance and result in other health problems such as those associated with obesity mentioned earlier. Electronic health records (EHR) would make the child s records available to his/her doctor at the point of care (POC) including the drug/medication history, which could reveal allergies, and past response to certain medications in terms of effectiveness and adverse reactions. Such information would no doubt help in planning treatment approaches in collaboration with the parents, and in an older child, with both. Researches have shown telephone-CBT whose use has increased since the 1990s, partly because of the introduction of 1-900 number counseling services and the greater use of telephone support services by insurance and medical groups, to be cost-effective for treating depression in adults and adolescents but its efficacy in children, remains less certain. Costs would even be less via Voice over Internet Protocol (VoIP), also called IP telephony, essentially an Internet-based phone network that enables individuals to make free long-distance phone calls using his/her computer. T-CBT could minimize worries about travel time, therapist availability, and transportation convenience and costs, and improve accessibility to care, in particular for patients who live in remote areas. Telemedicine is also a valuable ICT for CBT, offering similar benefits with the added advantage of visual contact with the therapist although this is also possible with Internet-based approaches such as VoIP. A recent research study published the September 2005 issue of Archives of General Psychiatry showed that patients with multiple sclerosis (MS) showed significant improvement in their depression during 16 weeks of T-CBT. According to the researchers, about two-thirds of depressed patients opt for psychotherapy over antidepressants, although only 10 to 45 percent ever make a first appointment and almost 50% drop out before completing the treatment often due to such problems as physical impairments, transportation difficulties, service accessibility, and time and monetary constraints, even stigma. Canadian researchers indicated, at the recent annual conference of the Canadian Congress of Neurological Sciences in Ottawa, that MS in children is more prevalent than previously thought; the diagnosis often missed due to its symptoms such as fatigue, being non-specific, and mistaken for chronic fatigue syndrome, even laziness. Children who have this condition, however, also experience acute relapses characterized by visual loss, numbness, weakness, or loss of balance, which would warrant not just immediate but long-term treatment. These children might also benefit from T-CBT or telehealth-enabled CBT. It is also important for the same physician to manage the child or barring this, for the child's medical history readily available to each new physician that treats him/her considering the variability in clinical presentation and the real chances of incomplete history with each new consultation. Here again we see the significance of healthcare ICT in qualitative healthcare delivery. Clearly, electronic medical records (EMR), would ensure the ready availability of crucial health information and would make communication and the sharing of such patient information, between the child's doctors possible and more efficient than say, via fax or by mail, the timeliness of the acquisition of such information possibly critical to the immediate outcome of the illness. Many parents probably by now know that depression could result in suicide even among children and adolescents. The increasing rates of ecstasy abuse by young people in many countries, has also been very much in the news. However, a recent population-based prospective study aimed at investigating whether symptoms of behavioral and emotional problems in childhood and early adolescence precede the use ecstasy (3, 4-methylenedioxymethamphetamine, MDMA), revealed an important link between these two health problems[10]. Conducted in the Dutch province of Zuid-Holland, among 1580 individuals, followed up across a 14-year period from childhood into adulthood, the researchers examined eight syndrome scales of childhood behavior. They found a significant association between scores in the deviant range for the scales designated as anxious or depressed in childhood and the use of MDMA in adolescents and adults, resulting in an increased risk. Conclusions from the study indicating that persons with childhood symptoms of anxiety and depression may have an increased tendency to use MDMA in adolescence or young adulthood, has significant implications for preventive and treatment policies regarding depression and MDMA. It is possible that persons with anxiety and depression are susceptible to the "positive" effects of MDMA, such as enhanced feelings of bonding with other people, euphoria, or relaxation. Should young people, parents, educators, healthcare professionals, and policy makers not have such crucial information? Would healthcare ICT not help in ensuring this awareness? How could incorporating health messages of this sort in the " Play Station " , X-Box " and other computer games facilitate their dissemination to target populations? Could such awareness not trigger efforts at preventing and/or treating depression and anxiety effectively in the first place? Could it not help promote bonding and affection between parents and their children thereby helping in some way to dissuade children from seeking solace and bonding in MDMA? Cigarette smoking is another major problem among young people whose prevalence ICT-enabled, targeted health campaigns could help to reduce. In the US, cigarette smoking is the single most preventable cause of morbidity and mortality, more deaths due to cigarette smoking than to AIDS, homicide, suicide, motor vehicle accidents, substance abuse (including alcohol, cocaine, and heroin), and fires combined. About 22% of U.S., high school students between ages 14 and 18 years smoke cigarettes and about 36% of youths aged 11 to 13 years have tried smoking, an early initiation that has been associated with a progression to other substance use. About a third of young people 18 years of age have tried smoking, and 3.1 million U.S. adolescents, or about 28%, smoke regularly, according to the Centers for Disease Control (CDC), the U.S. government establishing a number of programs aimed at preventing adolescent smoking to meet its Healthy People 2010 objective to reduce teen smoking to 16%. Cigarette smoking among youths is indeed, a global problem. Furthermore, in many parts of the world, the difference in current cigarette smoking between boys and girls is narrower than expected, according to an article published in The Lancet on February 17, 2006. In the Global Youth Tobacco Survey (GYTS), Charles Warren of the Centers for Disease Control and Prevention, and colleagues surveyed about 750,000 students aged 13¬15 years from 131 countries and the Gaza Strip and West Bank about tobacco use11. The survey revealed that almost 9% of students smoked, and 11% used tobacco products besides cigarettes currently. The survey also showed that the difference in current cigarette smoking between boys and girls is less than the difference between men and women, that 1 of 5 never-smokers reported being prone to smoking in the next year, over four of 10 students significantly exposed to secondhand smoke at home, and five of 10, in public places. According to the lead researcher, Dr. Warren, "Tobacco use is a major worldwide contributor to deaths from chronic diseases, and findings from the GYTS suggest current dire warnings that the annual death toll will double to 10 million by 2020 may be a conservative estimate. The true toll from tobacco use could be even greater with high rates of non-cigarette tobacco use and high rates of smoking among young girls." He adds, "Reduction of tobacco consumption will require a redoubling of efforts to prevent initiation and promote cessation among the large proportion of young people who currently use tobacco. High exposure to secondhand smoke suggests a need for countries to pass strong and effective smoke-free policies." Could one say more about the urgent need for targeted health campaigns? With a computer-savvy target population, and one increasingly formally educated even where computers are not so ubiquitous, efforts at such campaigns should aim towards maximizing the variety of multimedia communication channels via which young people access entertainment and sports, much as commercial advertisements reach them. UK MPs voted on February 14, 2006 to impose a ban on smoking in all enclosed public spaces, including pubs and restaurants with effect from summer 2007. Private homes, residential care homes, hospitals, prisons and hotel bedrooms are exempt from the ban whose violation attracts a £2,500 fine. There are concerns, among others that the ban would only make smokers move into the street, and smoke more at home, putting their health and of those in their households, including children, at even greater risk. Should the ban on smoking therefore not be total? Some local government authorities are in fact considering extending the ban. Dundee City and East Renfrewshire Council in Scotland for example, where the smoking ban is due to come into force on March 26, 2006 have also expressed interest in restricting smoking in parks, and to have smoke-free policies for areas used by children. The Scottish Executive and the Convention of Scottish Local Authorities (Cosla) have produced the Guidelines on the ban, stating, "Under the legislation, typically all wholly or substantially enclosed public premises used or visited by children either on their own or with their families or friends must be smoke-free". Second-hand smoking is not only unfair but also particularly harmful to the health of children and young people. As part of legislative efforts to promote health, and prevent illness, should children not be able to sue parents and relatives, or other persons that expose them to second-hand smoking? There are smoking-ban laws in other parts of the world too. In May 2004, Australia banned smoking on Manly one of the most famous and picturesque stretches of surfing beach in the country, a ban in other Sydney areas, including the world-famous Bondi Beach likely to follow. Australia has banned smoking in all airports, government offices, health clinics, and workplaces, with restaurants and shopping centers in most states and territories smoke-free. Ireland passed its anti-smoking legislation in March 2004, outlawing smoking in pubs, restaurants and other enclosed workplaces, violations costing up to 3,000 euros (£2,000) in fines. Recent laws in India have banned direct and indirect advertising of tobacco products and the sale of cigarettes to children. Tanzania banned smoking in many public places in July 2003, with public transport, schools, and hospitals declared smoke free zones. In Spain, a new law prohibiting smoking in offices, shops, schools, hospitals, cultural centers and on public transport came into effect on January 01, 200 6. Italy slammed a ban on smoking in all enclosed public places including bars and restaurants from midnight on January 10, 2005. Smoking rates in Canada are some of the lowest in the world, government statistics indicating some 21% of Canadians over the age of 15 years smoking in 2002. Some experts attribute the decline in smoking in the country to strict anti-smoking measures adopted in recent years, for examples outlawing smoking in workplaces and many public places, and graphic images of damage to internal organs by smoking on cigarette packets. In the US, many cities and states have anti-smoking legislation under consideration or already promulgated. In fact, California has some of the harshest and most elaborate anti-smoking laws anywhere in the world, with a ban on smoking inside or within one and a half meters of any public building since 1993, and recently extended to six meters, and smoking ban in restaurants, bars and enclosed workplaces, and on beaches, statewide. Smoking in bars, clubs, and restaurants has been illegal in New York since March 2003. Many other countries also have anti-smoking legislation in one form or another, although enforcing these laws is another matter in some of these countries, particularly in the developing world. These laws could help reduce the rates of smoking, including among young people, and protect children from the damaging effects of passive smoking. However, as much effort should go into enforcing the laws as with enacting them a process not always a cordial legislative exercise, but it would be difficult to enforce a law of which people are unaware. Here again, healthcare ICT could facilitate public awareness of such laws. Public information films "PIFs", were valuable media for health education, for example Sharon Osbourne and Kelly Holmes campaigning against bullying in Bullying-Tell Someone (2003). Her parents' heart attacks in their forties inspired Dr Rumeena Gujral's film, "Matters of Heart" or "Dil Ki Baatein", but this Bollywood style film is helping raise awareness about heart problems. British Asians are at a 50% increased risk of dying of a heart attack than the UK's White Europeans and at increased risk compared with Asians in Asia, the doctor said, causes including high fat diet and lack of exercise. "People can make very simple life style changes to try to reduce their risk. The film highlights some of these easy steps," she adds. "My parents were both diagnosed in their late 40s, and that was a real surprise, especially my mum who is quite slim. They did eat a traditional diet. They ate a lot of samosas and fried food. They were just eating a normal South Asian diet. But it was not until they had their problems that we noticed what was in the food, and the fact that as a group we tend to exercise less." Dr Gujral, a physician herself, hopes that the film, which the South Asian Health Foundation and Pfizer, commissioned and sponsored, respectively, will inspire better heart health by getting the message across more easily to the populations who need it. The above examples highlight how PIFS, even commercial films could help disseminate targeted health messages, and the need for the involvement of all stakeholders in this endeavor. Indeed, Dr Gujral hopes to do another film soon about diabetes, before going back to medicine and train in accident and emergency. Not only is there a variety of technologies that could also help in this regard, progress in ICT research will likely offer even more cost-effective opportunities for information diffusion in future.

Advances in information technologies are indeed improving our knowledge and offering new vistas for treating a variety of health problems including those that affect young people. Recent bioinformatics research published in the November 11, 2005 issue of the journal, Science has identified a novel anti-obesity hormone[12]. Ghrelin, a peptide hormone that induces appetite, derived from a larger protein, a prohormone, through posttranslational processing, researchers presuming that they could derive another hormone, with an exact opposite property, which is capable of suppressing appetite. Their search of the complete GenBank database with the total prohormone sequence yielded a second region on the prohormone gene conserved across 11 species. The researchers named it ghrelin-associated peptide "obestatin", additional research showing that it suppressed food intake, gastrointestinal function, and decreased body weight in rats. No doubt, future research will elucidate more of the characteristics of this prohormone system in human body-weight regulation. This prohormone might in fact hold the key to weight control in children in the near future. Imaging studies are also helping redirect thinking on targeted health education campaigns. Preliminary findings of an ongoing study at the Universite de Montreal using magnetic resonance images (MRI) to measure the reaction of the brain's prefrontal cortex in the right hemisphere to the graphic ads on cigarette packs showing images of necrotic hearts and lungs, damages due to cigarette smoking caused, are instructive. The ads aimed at discouraging people from smoking but the findings indicate that they only affect non-smokers, smokers not taking notice. The researchers studied twelve young female smokers and an equal number of non-smokers, exposed to 15 of the 16 photos on cigarette packages in Canada since 2001. The exposure caused an instant neuron activity in the dorsolateral part of the prefrontal cortex and the amygdale cortices, the right prefrontal cortex in control of negative emotions. The researchers found no activation of the region linked with aversion on volunteers seeing the photos, as there should if aversion occurred with the photos or text ads such as "Cigarettes hurt babies," and "Cigarettes leave you breathless". The researchers concluded that the ads could prevent non-smokers from starting, but not make smokers quit smoking. These findings certainly have implications for targeted health campaigns. For example, would it be more effective to target ads at young people suggesting that it is lousy to try to kiss someone with smelly, rotten, teeth, or to ask them to imagine what someone could think of them with a foul smell of stale tobacco in their breath when chatting with them? Young people are in general impressionable. This makes the prospects of appropriate health campaigns directed at this population achieving the desired results quite high. However, the campaigns would need to consider the most appropriate media and no doubt; information technologies would be ideal, after all many of these young people grew up with the technologies and are comfortable using them. Besides health education campaigns, healthcare ICT deployment in preventing diseases and promoting wellness in children and adolescents could help reduce health spending, which is soaring in many developed countries at alarming rates. In the US for example, $1 out of every $5 spent in the U.S. economy will go for health care within the next ten year, with annual spending consistently growing faster than the overall economy, according to the US government in a February 21 2006 statement. Increased spending on hospital care, home health services, drugs and public health programs will increase total health care spending from its current 16.2% of the economy to 20% in 2015, according to Centers for Medicare and Medicaid Services projections, compared to all of manufacturing's current 20% of the economy. Rising health care spending could also swell the numbers of the uninsured, which could adversely influence the state of the country's overall health, including that of its economy. If there were cost-control measures likely to change that trend, the increased implementation of healthcare ICT would be one of them. Consider that the US will spend $4 trillion on health care, or about $12,320 per person annually, by 2015. In addition to its ongoing upward spiral in healthcare costs, Hurricanes Rita and Katrina acutely increased government spending on public health, with the Federal public health program spending increasing 24.3% to $11.3 billion in 2005, compared with 5.7% in 2004, disaster relief the principal reason. The federal government s portion of prescription drug spending will also rise from 2% in 2005 to 27% in 2006, as the new Medicare drug program takes over payments from state Medicaid programs and from seniors who formerly paid for their own medications. Private health insurance premiums increased 6.8% in 2005, although not as much as in 2002, when premiums peaked at 11.5%, a decline expected to cease by 2007, when premiums will increase quicker[13]. The need to control health spending in the US is understandable considering these figures. Health spending in many other developed countries has also been rising. In Canada for example, Medicare will likely consume over half of total revenues from all sources in seven of 10 provinces by the year 2022, according to the most recent five-year trends in a Fraser Institute release on October 31, 2005. The report also noted that were the relative speed of health spending and revenue growth not to slow down, public health care spending would guzzle two thirds of total revenues in these provinces by the year 2032, and ultimately 100 per cent by 2050. Short-and long-term trends reveal a faster growth rate of health spending on average than total revenue in all provinces, indeed faster than inflation and economic growth, health care is thus gulping a greater than ever portion of provincial revenues over time. Ontario is the worst hit, its public health spending expected to surpass 50% of revenue in 2011, up to two-thirds of revenue by 2017 and 100% by the end of 2026 if the trends persist. Prince Edward Island, New Brunswick, British Columbia, Manitoba, Saskatchewan, and Newfoundland and Labrador follow, their public health spending unlikely to exceed 50% of revenues until another 12years to 17 years, Nova Scotia, Alberta, and Quebec, even much later, actually not until 2061 in Quebec. Tax increases and oil play significant roles in Nova Scotia/Quebec and Alberta, respectively, skewing the estimates, and raising sustainability issues. Provinces might even reach the 50% mark sooner considering the interest cost of servicing the accumulated debt in each province a fixed expense, with resultant shrinkage in total revenues available for health programs spending. The graying of the population could also jerk up health spending as could measures to reduce wait times. There is no doubt that healthcare costs are higher treating the chronic health problems that frequently come with age but healthcare ICT could help minimize both of these costs in a number of ways, including via targeted health programs for young persons, which would make it likelier that they would grow into healthier adults with less chronic health problems. Healthcare ICT could also facilitate the prevention of the long-term consequences of health problems even in young persons by enabling the early diagnosis and prompt treatment of these health problems and helping to reduce the chances of their long-term sequelae via adequate and effective rehabilitation programs. There are a number of issues such as availability and distribution of healthcare professionals, and their related issues such as remuneration policies, and the accessibility to health services, among others involved in solving the wait-times problem. Healthcare ICT could also help reduce the severity of the problems that these issues pose. Data mining technologies for example could help unveil cryptic salient facts about service usage that could help in the optimization of scarce resources. Telehealth of various sorts could alleviate the problems of physician misdistribution and improve access to care. EHR and EMR would facilitate communication between doctors and rationalize the referral process. Healthcare-ICT enabled primary, secondary, and tertiary prevention would help reduce disease prevalence, morbidity, and mortality, reducing the burden of disease on various facets of the health system. Regulatory measures for example mandating the publication of surgical wait lists would indicate where it is most appropriate to refer patients so that some specialists' wait list are not mounting while other specialists are idle. There may also be a need to offer incentive to surgeons for extra efforts to clear up wait lists, and to encourage family doctors and indeed, all doctors to implement relevant healthcare ICT in order to improve the efficiency of their operations. It is true that some high-tech equipments are expensive. However, could the benefits of such investments not far outweigh their costs even if only in the long term? Would it not reassure the various entities involved in health care provision that there is no long any need to worry about adverse selection or moral hazard with most people relatively healthy and physically fit? Would there still be need to worry about escalating hospitalization and medication costs when fewer people are admitted into hospitals or are even ill and require medications in the first place? These are achievable objectives although they may sound utopian on first consideration. However, considering how Komatsu, with less than 35% in sales than Caterpillar in 1970 and few if any market outside Japan, manufacturing only small bulldozers became in 1985 a $2.8 billion behemoth with a product range including industrial robots, and earth-moving equipments, posing a challenge to the industry leader, would make clear what strategic intent could accomplish over time. More recently, Juniper networks, an upstart computer hardware firm, is gaining increasing access into the core router market of the massive Cisco. Indeed, such strategic intent, applied to health should serve as the rallying focus for achieving the seemingly impossible task of controlling and curtailing the runaway healthcare costs with which many developed countries currently struggle. Consider the effects of the following on the health costs. 15-year old Tanya is on treatment for depression with an antidepressant, say a selective serotonin reuptake inhibitor (SSRI.) Somewhere down the road, she develops a chest infection after a few days of what she thought was a cold, and would soon go away. The ER doctor who saw her at almost midnight when her parents rushed her to the hospital, prescribed linezolid (Zyvoxam), the first of the oxazolidones, a new class of antibiotics, and a weak reversible monoamine oxidase inhibitor (MAOI). MAOIs are a group of antidepressants used commonly to treat atypical depression. Tanya's psychiatrist is unaware of the new prescription and the ER doctor of the prescribed SSRI. The young woman develops the serotonin syndrome the next day. First described in 1959 in a patient with tuberculosis who received meperidine, the patient, who showed clonus, severe muscular hyperactivity, and was extremely rigid, later died, the cause of death stated as "fatal toxic encephalitis". Later observations revealed that the administration of two or more medications that elevated serotonin concentrations resulted in a similar constellation of symptoms characterized by high fever, mental status, neuromuscular, and behavioral changes, termed the serotonin syndrome in 1982. Tanya had high fever, sweating, and tremors. She was restless, confused and had myoclonus. Her parents rushed her back to the ER, and after rigorous questioning of her parents, the ER doctor diagnosed the syndrome. The doctor discontinued her medications among other instant measures including aggressively reducing her body temperature, and admitted her into hospital. Serotonin syndrome can be life threatening, but Tanya's symptoms resolved over the next day or two, and the doctors discharged her on the morning of the third day. This example underlines the value of the electronic health records (EHR) systems, and of computerized physician order entry (CPOE). For some reason, the first ER doctor did not ask Tanya and her parents the medications she was using. Tanya and her parents did not also tell the doctor that she was on an antidepressant. Despite this circumstance, the ER doctor could still have found out that Tanya was on an antidepressant if the hospital had EHR, and the Psychiatrist had electronic medical records (EMR) and both systems could communicate with each other. The ER doctor would have gained instant access to Tanya's health records at the click of a mouse, including her medication history. If the hospital had CPOE, it would have alerted the ER doctor to the potential drug interactions that resulted in the life-threatening hyperserotonergic syndrome Tanya suffered. Scientists at Pfizer, which makes Linezolid, are in fact warning doctors to watch for signs of serotonin syndrome in patients that are receiving the sort of concomitant treatments Tanya had. This is despite the firm not having any evidence of an increase in serotonin syndrome among patients taking the combination although it acknowledges the potential for interaction citing nine publications in the warning of post-marketing cases of the syndrome over the past three years. How many patients' lives could healthcare providers implementing these technologies have saved that had life-threatening complications of drug-drug interactions of this sort? How much could efforts to prevent such morbidities, and in some cases even fatalities resulting from not preventing such interactions save in human and material costs? Did Tanya need hospitalization for three days for example, if she did not have the syndrome and how much savings could have accrued from not hospitalizing her? This example also illustrates the need for patients to have health information, and to be willing to volunteer the information. Indeed, Tanya could have had her own personal health records (PHR), from which the ER doctor could also have accessed her health information online, with her consent, of course. Incidentally, there is evidence for the increasing acceptance of electronic storage and transmission of health records by the public particularly with the efforts of both software/ICT vendors to improve security technologies, and of government to legislate the safety, confidentiality, and security of patient information. Even cell phones used by doctors reduce the rate of medical errors or injury, according to a recent study by researchers at the Yale School of Medicine. The first report to demonstrate the beneficial effect of mobile phones on patient safety, the findings, published in Anesthesia and Analgesia, were of an analysis of 4,018 responses from attendees at the 2003 meeting of the American Society of Anesthesiologists to a five-question survey. Asked about the communication means the anesthetists used in the operating room/intensive care unit and their experiences with communications delays and medical errors, 65% reported using pagers, 17%, cell phones. Forty percent of the former reported communication delays compared to 31% of the latter. Cell phones also reduced medical error and injury rates due to communication delays, the 2.4% prevalence of electronic interference with life support devices, for example, ventilators, much less than the 14.9% communication delay-related medical error risk. The cell phone serves other purposes, for examples, patients could use it to book an appointment to see the doctor, and doctors could send important lab results via text messaging to their patients, which in some studies, helped reduce time to receive treatments, minimizing morbidities and saving costs. There are also cell phones capable of measuring blood alcohol levels, making it possible for youngsters, for example, to know when to stop drinking, and when not to drive after having been drinking. This no doubt could help prevent road traffic accidents and the injuries, possibly even deaths that result from driving under the influence (DUI.) of alcohol. Personal digital assistants (PDAs) are also increasingly valuable ICT devices for doctors, most with a variety of third-party applications, for example, epocrates, which provides doctors with valuable medication information on the go, which could enhance patient safety. Others even come bundled with e-mail, productivity, and multimedia software, facilitating doctor-patient communication. Pocket PC, the generic name for Windows Mobile PDAs, have pocket versions of Microsoft applications such as Microsoft Word, Excel, and Outlook, enabling synchronization with Microsoft Outlook on a Windows PC, and it has Windows Media Player for multimedia content. These and newer technologies will play an even greater role over time as more doctors embrace healthcare ICT as invaluable practice tools.

The US government spends more per person than the mix of public and private expenditures in the UK, which latter also provides free health care for all residents, even if US health spending is only on the elderly with Medicare, and the poor, with Medicaid. Some would even argue that the US spends more on health per person worldwide considering health insurance costs on government employees and tax breaks to promote private health care, among others. There are some who advocate cost sharing in health services provision in both the US and Canada as one way to reduce government health spending, an idea that has the power of the discerning patient at its core. However, the discerning patient must first be an informed individual for him/her to make the best choices regarding health care provision, including when to make the trip to the family doctor, which specialist to patronize, and how much to spend on healthcare. This again underscores the value of healthcare ICT, with an array of technologies that could furnish individuals with the right information when needed, in the new healthcare dispensation. The increasing use of information technologies in health will certainly influence other stakeholders in the industry, for example, the health insurance industry. Would the statistical computations and probability analyses of the health insurance industry continue to hold for example in a milieu of certain medical knowledge, for example that genetic mapping provides regarding who has what disease long before the individual even manifests its symptoms? How would such information affect the delicate balance among the key health industry players, the determination of premiums, the health benefits companies pay, how much government spends on health, and on projections for health expenditures in ten, twenty, even thirty years? How could such information, obtained since birth for example, or possibly even before, determine the health services provision the child would need? Would it not be possible to plan healthcare utilization by the child through his/her life span right from birth?

How could such planning influence efforts to gain firmer control over health spending in the near future? Could such information also not give individuals more power over their health, and by extension, their lives? Would individuals for example not be able to plan how many children to have, living in which environment could be inimical to their health, or whether to avoid marrying certain persons whose genetic makeup would result in major health problems for their children, if they had any? Would this sort of rational choices not help improve health and well-being and reduce health spending? Health policy makers no doubt constantly examine issues germane to policy formulation, for example looking at strengthening community-based care for youths with or at risk of behavioral health disorders, or extending telehealth pediatric services to a remote rural community to avoid disrupting school attendance by chronically ill children whose parents would have to take to hospitals far from home otherwise. Such telehealth services incidentally would also decrease family needs, caregiver strain, and parents' missed workdays. The emergence of new health services paradigms that advances in healthcare information technologies would warrant is likely to change significantly the approaches to such policy exercises. For example, a recent pilot study set out to compare emergency department (ED) cost and utilization by members enrolled in a pilot program designed to reduce the use of hospital EDs with the costs and utilization incurred by a control group. The researchers noted that in the one-year period following to program initiation, the average per member per month cost for ED utilization of the intervention group was $1.36 less than that of the control group, although there was no significant difference regarding per-visit cost related to ED utilization. This suggests that the savings accrued due to a reduction in ED visits, rather than from reduced cost per visit. Children in the intervention group visited the ED on the average about eight fewer times per thousand members per month than the control group, with still no significant difference in the overall (ED and non-ED) care costs between the two groups. The researchers concluded that analysis from the first year of this pilot program indicates that providing enhanced, coordinated, primary care access to Medicaid children significantly reduced the ED use among healthy children, but the overall cost of care remained unchanged[14]. Other studies have reported the association of increases in Medicaid health maintenance organization (HMO) enrollment with less emergency room use, more outpatient visits, fewer hospitalizations, higher rates of reporting having put off care, and lower satisfaction with the most recent visit. Studies have also linked Medicaid primary care case management (PCCM) plans with increases in outpatient visits, but also with increased rates of reporting unmet medical needs, putting off care, and lacking usual care sources. Could such findings not influence policy decision making regarding service provision for children, for example providing more primary care access? Would proposed service changes not require a thorough examination of the role healthcare ICT would play in facilitating the communication and sharing of patient information in real time at the points of care (POC) in disparate health services locations? Immunizations are crucial aspects of child healthcare. Healthcare information systems are not just important to implementing immunization programs, the consistency and quality of immunization monitoring systems could be crucial to the success or otherwise of the programs. Healthcare ICT plays an important role in ensuring the proper verification of doses administered at the peripheral health services levels for instance by facilitating the communication and sharing of accurate and timely information between health units and their districts. Appropriate deployment, maintenance, and standardized data quality audits (DQAs) could help prevent deficiencies in the monitoring systems. This could prevent problems such as the inconsistent use of monitoring charts, defective monitoring of vaccine stocks, injection supplies, reporting accuracy and promptness, and of adverse events reporting, among others, problems that could severely compromise immunization programs and put the lives of children in jeopardy. Developments in the technology industry are also important determinants of the direction of child and adolescent health services, and of all healthcare services for that matter. For example, the fate of BlackBerry, the popular wireless e-mail device, remains uncertain as a US federal judge ended a hearing on February 23, 2006 without making a ruling on an injunction request in a patent infringement suit that NTP Inc., a small patent-holding firm based in Arlington company filed against Research In Motion (RIM) Ltd. of Waterloo, Ontario. Owners of BlackBerry including healthcare professionals will therefore remain in limbo, many concerned about the prospects of having to discard the device if future court rulings against RIM were unfavorable. There is also uncertainty about how the lingering war between PDA devices running PalmSource operating system (OS) and those based on Microsoft handheld OS over market share would play out, particularly in the health industry where these devices are gaining increasing currency. There are conflicts elsewhere in the hardware market for example in the enterprise market, with storage networking technologies at loggerheads, and UNIX-, Windows-, and Linux-based systems engaged in fierce server OS competition, and in the disk drive market, Seagate Technology and Maxtor compete in similarly stiff price wars. With regard the hardware industry in particular, these intense price wars may buttress the claims by some regarding the commoditization of hardware, but perhaps more importantly for the health industry, could drive prices down sufficiently to trigger a massive healthcare ICT diffusion in the industry. Such pervasive deployment of health information technologies would augur well for the disease prevention, health promotion, and population health agenda of the health services, and would help reduce the overall costs of healthcare delivery and facilitate in tandem, the emergence of an inclusive and qualitative healthcare delivery system. Government on its part would need to continue playing the pivotal role it has in laying the technology infrastructure necessary for the full exploitation of the potential benefits of healthcare ICT, and in helping tease out some of the important technical issues holding this back via the provision of funds for research and the promotion of intersectoral collaboration. For example, Larry Ellison, chairperson and CEO of Oracle, not long ago advocated the creation of a national ID card system in the US as a way to address airport security in the wake of the September 11 terrorist attacks. According to Ellison, "We need a national ID card with our photograph and thumbprint digitized and embedded in the ID card" even offering to "provide the software for this absolutely free." Although the Bush administration has rejected the idea of a national ID, some US Congressmen actually considered taking Ellison up on his offer. Not exactly a new idea, having come up as a possible antidote to illegal immigration in the mid-1990s, and in debates over gun control, social security, and health reforms, its application in the latter continues to generate intense debate even today. Not only have advances in technologies, for example, the emergence of biometrics, helped allay the fears of some regarding the security of national ID cards, the urgent need to implement electronic health records, nationally, with the huge investments infused into various projects to actualize which also necessitating resolving the matter once and for all. A variety of cutting-edge technologies such as extensive computer databases/registries, digital fingerprinting, facial recognition systems, software data collection and voice authentication technologies, electronic retinal and handprint scans, and a variety of other technologies are already on the market, their adoption advocated by proponents with Olympian zeal. However, besides issues relating to security, abuse, and fraud, they continue to encounter equally passionate opposition by civil liberties advocates. People are even more concerned about these issues when it comes to personal health information. Yet, implicit in the seamless and effective operations of any national health information network is the assumption that disparate health information networks, for example, the current regional health information organizations (RHIO) would not just be able to "speak" with one another, but also be able to recognize who they are speaking about and that it is the same person. Some argue that the best way to achieve these goals would be for each person to have an identifier. Besides ensuring the interoperability of information networks, the problem is that an identifier error could end up perpetrated throughout the entire system ad infinitum, some contend. One cannot gainsay the likely consequences of such an error in terms of patient safety and escalating healthcare and system maintenance and repair costs. Such issues continue to hinder the timely implementation of national health information networks in the US and other countries with similar plans, and would continue to demand utmost attention from particularly those involved with the technical aspects of ICT implementation in the health industry. There is little doubt that appropriate solutions would soon emerge however, and that the march of technology into the healthcare arena would continue apace.

References

1. Reilly JJ, Dorosty AR. Epidemic of obesity in UK children. *Lancet* 1999; 354: 1874-5

2. Reilly JJ, Armstrong J, Dorosty AR, Emmett PM, Ness A, Rogers I, Steer C, Sherriff A, for the Avon Longitudinal Study of Parents and Children Study Team
Early life risk factors for obesity in childhood: cohort study
BMJ, Jun 2005; 330: 1357.

3. Dietz WH. Birth weight, socioeconomic class, and adult adiposity among African Americans. *Am J Clin Nutr* 2000; 72: 335-6

4. Birch LL, Fisher JO. Development of eating behaviors among children and adolescents. *Pediatrics* 1998; 101: 539-49.

5. Dabelea D, Hanson RL, Lindsay RS, Pettitt DJ, Imperatore G, Gabir MM, et al. Intrauterine exposure to diabetes conveys risks for type 2 diabetes and obesity: a study of discordant sibships. *Diabetes* 2000; 49: 2208-11

6. Fries AB et. al. Early experience in human is associated with changes in neuropeptides critical for regulating social behavior. *Proc Natl Acad Sci* USA 2005 Nov 22; 102: 17237-40.

7. Carter CS. The chemistry of child neglect: Do oxytocin and vasopressin mediate the effects of early experience? *Proc Natl Acad Sci* USA 2005 Dec 20; 102: 18247-8.

8. *Nature* 2004; 429: 754

9. March J, Silva S, Petrycki S, Curry J et. al. Fluoxetine, cognitive-behavioral therapy, and their combination for adolescents with depression: Treatment for

Adolescents with Depression Study (TADS) randomized controlled trial. *JAMA* 2004 Aug 18; 292(7):807-20.

10. Huizink AC, Ferdinand RF, van der Ende J, & Verhulst FC. Symptoms of anxiety and depression in childhood and use of MDMA: prospective, population based study. *BMJ*, 24 February 2006.

11. Warren CW, Jones NR, Eriksen MP, Asma S. Patterns of Global Tobacco Use Among Young People And Implications For Future Chronic Disease Burden In Adults. *Lancet* 2006; S0140-6736(06)68192-0. Available at http://www.thelancet.com/journals/eop Accessed on February 25, 2006

12. Zhang JV et al. Obestatin, a peptide encoded by the ghrelin gene, opposes ghrelin's effects on food intake. *Science* 2005 Nov 11; 310: 996-9

13. Available at:

http://www.medicalnewstoday.com/healthnews.php?newsid=38133
Accessed on February 25, 2006

14. Wang C. Villar ME. Mulligan DA. Hansen T. Cost and utilization analysis of a pediatric emergency department diversion project. *Pediatrics*. 116(5):1075-9, 2005 Nov.

15. Baker LC. Afendulis C. Medicaid managed care and health care for children. *Health Services Research*. 40(5 Pt 1):1466-88, 2005 Oct.

ICT & Men's Health

Consumer-driven healthcare is increasingly in the news. This healthcare delivery model aims to empower the individual healthcare consumer in many ways, including among others being able to choose healthcare providers. However, the story does not end there. An integral aspect of this model is the concept of cost sharing, wherein the consumer pays part of the incurred healthcare costs. The idea is that this would make healthcare consumers more discerning in their utilization of health services. By becoming more astute, seeking the best services at the most affordable costs, market forces would compel health care providers to improve their services and offer new ones to enhance their competitiveness, and prices would likely fall, reducing overall healthcare costs. Recent developments in the US health scene indicate interest in and support for this model, for example the signing into law by President Bush the Medicare law creating the Health Savings Account (HSA) on December 8, 2003[1]. The law, modeled after the medical savings account (MSA) expansion that Rep. Bill Archer, Chairman of the House Ways and Means Committee, announced on September 20, 2000, continues to generate controversy even as statistics show more employers offering and more Americans signing up for HSA[2]. Indeed HSA has been controversial since the Health Insurance Portability and Accountability Act of 1996 (HIPAA) offered small employers and the self-employed a new option in health care coverage termed a medical savings account (MSA), hoping that it would reduce health insurance premiums and enable the insured to accumulate tax favored funds to pay for out-of-pocket medical expenses. To be sure, several states have run MSA-type programs for up to a decade before then, but the HIPAA was the first federal program allowing federal tax breaks on the savings accounts established for medical purposes. An HSA, a savings account established by self-employed persons or employers on behalf their employees, which the insured person controls to pay health care expenses works in combination with a high-deductible health plan (HDHP.) The insurance plan pays the rest of an insured's medical expenses during the year, if qualified medical expenses for that year exceeded the deductible and total out-of-pocket maximum. There are thus eligibility criteria for HSA, for examples "1st dollar" medical benefits such as Medicare, Tricare Coverage, Flexible Spending Arrangements (FSA), and Health Reimbursement Arrangements (HRA) make someone ineligible for an HSA. Some of these, for example the restrictions on HSA/HRA/FSA combinations, and other eligibility criteria remain contentious, but perhaps even more so are issues relating to and in particular, the limits placed on the HDHP. Many believe for example that HSA only favors the rich that could afford HDHP. Others argue that the limits on HDHP, health insurance plan with minimum deductible of, for 2006, $1,050 (self-only coverage) and $2,100 (family coverage), amounts indexed annually for inflation; and annual out-of-pocket (including deductibles and co-pays) that cannot exceed, for 2006, of $5,250 (self-only coverage) and $10,500 (family coverage), also indexed annually for inflation, are unrealistic for chronically ill individuals. They also argue that the HSAs would be inadequate in case of a catastrophic illness, prolonged hospitalization, or a mostly unhealthy year. It was perhaps in response to these criticisms of HSA that President Bush announced in his 2006 State of the Union Speech increases in the amount allowed to accumulate in existing health savings account. Indeed, the President also touched on a variety of related issues in the speech, for examples, providing, further tax breaks for individuals that purchase private insurance on their own, and more portability for health insurance when people change jobs. Others included the provision of easier access to information regarding physician pricing and quality, promoting the adoption of electronic medical records, and limiting non-economic damages in malpractice verdicts. According to Al Hubbard, chair of Bush's National Economic Council, "The American people are very, very frustrated with the health care system, for good reason" "All we're doing is trying to give consumers the opportunity to be engaged in the process.......It's not fair for people who feel like they can't leave their job or they'd lose their insurance. And it's not fair not to know what the quality of the providers is, and what kind of pricing they're being charged for services." The question some are asking is how fair it is to transfer much of the cost of health care to the consumer, a move they argue would discourage people, especially poor people, from seeking healthcare. Others insist that despite its perceived flaws, preliminary data from a report by America's Health Insurance Plans indicate an increase in enrollment in HSAs to three million, tripling over the last 10 months3. This seeming interest in HSA brings to the fore a fundamental issue pertaining to consumer-driven healthcare delivery model, that of consumers being able to make the right choices lacking the basic information to help them make those choices. The consumer-driven healthcare model is also of interest in Canada. On February 28, 2006, the Alberta government announced that it has developed the framework for its "Third Way" health care reforms, including a plan that allows patients to pay cash for quicker access to some non-emergency procedures. According to Health Minister Iris Evans, "What we're looking for is some middle ground that accounts for capacity to keep the public system strong and protected by sufficient doctors. You can talk about it being two-tiered, "..It's no different that what's going on in every place they have private clinics. It's people making choices for themselves." The Quebec government also recently announced plans to allow its residents to seek healthcare in the private sector, albeit in a limited form, in compliance with a 2005 Supreme Court ruling, although its doctors do not have the option of switching back and forth between public and private systems hence must choose one or the other. Alberta's Third Way plan encompasses ten policies, namely, putting patients at the centre, promoting flexibility in the scope of practice of health professionals, implementing new compensation models, strengthening inter-regional collaboration, and reshaping the role of hospitals. Others are establishing parameters for publicly funded health services, creating long-term sustainability and flexible funding options, expanding system capacity, paying for choice and access while protecting the public system, and deriving economic benefits from health services and research. Under the Alberta plan, patients would be able to pay for some non-emergency procedures, such as knee or hip surgeries, and doctors, to practice in both public and private health care systems. Another reform in the province aims to expand alternatives for private health

139

insurance on treatments that may not have coverage in future, including emerging technologies and medications that Alberta Health does not cover, and yet another, to free doctors by creating options for nurses and pharmacists to make clinical care and treatment decisions. The government hopes that these reforms would reduce hospital wait times, and plans to pursue them despite concerns by some that doctors working in both sectors would likely ultimately deplete the public health sector of scarce resources. According to the province's Premier, Ralph Klein, "The health system must change to survive, and all premiers agree on that. The federal health minister agrees." In response to the announcement, the Federal Health Minister Tony Clement noted that he would study the health care reforms. He added, "The question I have is the same question that Albertans will be asking -- how does any particular solution that is posed by the government of Alberta ensure that accessibility in the public system will not only be maintained but enhanced?" Indeed, accessibility to care is one of the key pillars of the Canada Health Act, one more pervasive deployment of information technologies would no doubt help accomplish, and on which governments in Canada, at all levels are investing substantially and increasingly in appreciation of this fact. Similar consumer-driven health reforms are underway in many other developed countries for examples the UK and some other European countries, and in Australia, and New Zealand. These developments underscore an appreciation of the key role of healthcare ICT in the success of the consumer-driven, healthcare model, or any healthcare delivery model for that matter. Considering not only that the health industry is one of the most information-intensive but also that the communication and sharing of patient information is at the core of medical practice, including patient treatment, this appreciation was inevitable, hence expected. Healthcare stakeholders need to continue to appreciate these important facts, and there is increasing evidence that many do. At a Capitol Hill briefing on February 13, 2006, health insurance industry leaders emphasized how the industry is providing healthcare value added services to employers, health care practitioners and in particular, consumers, via health insurance plans' cutting-edge information technology (IT) strategies. They noted that health insurance plans are not just utilizing IT to facilitate claims processing, but also to promote evidence-based care and empower consumers by providing them access to improved information and decision tools. According to Karen Ignagni, President, and CEO of America's Health Insurance Plans (AHIP), "Health insurance plans are spearheading efforts to improve the value of health care services and are delivering tangible solutions for consumers and physicians through an array of health IT advances". She added, "Health insurance plans are investing in health IT because they recognize the improvements that can be achieved in promoting effective and quality health care". Ms. Ignagni introduced three industry leaders at the briefing whose organizations are making notable contributions to healthcare ICT. They include, Vicky Gregg, President, and CEO of BlueCross BlueShield of Tennessee, who discussed Community Connection, a novel program that facilitates care promotion among Medicaid beneficiaries, and creates a patient-based community health record giving timely access to an individual's health records via a secure Web site to disparate providers treating the individual. Jerry Senne, CEO of Health First Health Plans Inc., mentioned the VitalWatch system, an electronic intensive care unit (ICU) already implemented in three Florida hospitals. Dr. Reed Tuckson, Senior Vice President of Consumer Health and Medical Care Advancement at UnitedHealth Group talked about his firm's user-friendly consumer Web site and its plan to provide personal health records (PHR) to members nationwide. Other private sector organizations are tapping opportunities the need for health information to help consumers make the right choices regarding and to facilitate health services provision create, for example WebMD Health, a key medical information Web site, which on February 27, 2006, announced plans to assist individuals enrolled in employer health plans store their personal health information securely online. The company indicates that it has signed contracts with major health insurers and employers to operate private-access Web sites where employees can keep track of their medical records, search information on diseases, and compare and contrast costs and ratings for doctors and hospitals. The company would receive licensing fees from employers or their insurers depending on the services it provides and the number of health plan members. WebMD says it has signed multiyear licensing contracts with major health insurers including Cigna, Aetna, and WellPoint, and several large employers such as Cisco Systems, Dell Computer, Bank of America, IBM, Shell Oil, and Pfizer, as well as the state of North Carolina, and is negotiating with banks and financial institutions such as Fidelity. With the WebMD service, employees would be able to complete health status questionnaires on its Web sites, and with some contracts, such as those with Pfizer, Dell, and North Carolina, able to merge the answers with medical payment data from visits to their doctors and hospitalizations, hence to create personal health histories. They would also receive reminders for periodic checkups, and online alerts regarding problems requiring urgent attention. Indeed, many financial institutions consider this consumer-driven healthcare model, in which WebMD clearly seems poised to play an active role, a great chance to manage health savings accounts (HSA) that employers are increasingly offering their workers. It remains unclear how the personal health profiles that WebMD creates, drawing on medical billing claims, will fare with the emergence of databases of detailed electronic medical records (EMR) that the US Federal government is promoting and investing substantially on for patient safety, and to reduce health spending, among others.

Not too long ago, there was little indication of an imminent increasingly positive public attitude toward the idea of personal health records (PHR). With the negative publicity heaved on the problem of identity theft, the menace of hackers, and fears about the privacy and possible abuse of health information, the skepticism of the public regarding virtual storage of personal health records was not surprising. Nonetheless, times seem to be changing. The Washington Post on March 15, 2005, examined the mounting popularity of PHR in the US as Americans seek ways to consolidate their health information, with more firms offering PHR services, convinced that more Americans, in particular those that have chronic diseases and those who care for children and aging parents, will soon demand digital, all-inclusive medical records. While healthcare providers in the main own and control electronic health records (EHR), although they still need consent from patients to share health information, patients own and have more control over their PHR. Sponsors of PHR services, including health plans and hospitals, charge as little as $44.95 to store a patient's medical information on a CD and $24.95, online. For example, subscribers to the Maryland-based Laxor's system could upload their health information including on illnesses, treatments, medications, allergies, blood-pressure readings, doctor visits, and test results to a secure Web site, accessible to them and to whomever they authorize. The system, set up and managed by personal health information managers, could also remind subscribers of doctor's appointments and screening tests. FollowMe, another sponsor, provides an e-mail account, printable emergency card with photo ID, and direct links to information sources and enables uploading of laboratory and diagnostic scans. WebMD's system additionally offers health news and customized content and tools. Besides increasing competition among sponsors, which would likely further reduce subscription costs, sponsors face the prospects of legal challenges on privacy issues, and with the perpetrators of identity theft and hackers still out there, some believe that it is a matter of time before these issues surface. The increasing interest in patient information demonstrates more awareness of the capabilities of healthcare ICT in healthcare delivery. An aspect of this interest that needs even further attention concerns health information that patients need to prevent illnesses, and stay healthy, and when they are ill, to know what to do, where to seek medical help, and what to expect regarding the outcomes of their illnesses. There is much information on the World Wide Web currently purporting to serve these important purposes but that in fact are creating more problems for people than they solve. Many of such information are inaccurate, stale, and biased toward the marketing objectives of the owners of the Web sites on which they appear. One could not overemphasize the dangers involved in these situations for the unsuspecting individual. No doubt, the rate at which medical information changes could be intimidating to even healthcare professionals, although it is not necessarily a bad thing that new knowledge emerges that fast. Indeed, progress in medical knowledge is not only desirable, it is imperative for us to stand any chance of achieving our goals of improving health service provision, disease prevention, health promotion, and superior overall population health. The problem is harnessing the power of healthcare ICT to sieve this information and channel the right information to the right population at the right time. Most people for example already know the benefits of Cocoa in reducing the risks of heart diseases, known in fact since at least the 18th century, but researchers are just starting to collate scientific evidence to back these claims, and they now have more compelling evidence that cocoa is indeed, good for your heart. Dutch scientists recently observed that elderly men who consumed cocoa had lower blood pressure levels, and were less likely to die from cardiovascular problems. The Dutch scientists, from the National Institute for Public Health and the Environment in Bilthoven, who published their findings in the February 27, 2006 issue of the Archives of Internal Medicine4, studied 470 men aged 65 to 84 years. The men had physical examinations and interviews regarding their dietary intake when they enrolled in the study in 1985 and at follow-up visits five and ten years later. Over the next 15 years, men who consumed cocoa repeatedly had significantly lower blood pressure than those who did not. Three hundred and fourteen men died, 152 due to cardiovascular diseases, during the study period, men in the group with the highest cocoa consumption with 50% reduction in risk of death of these diseases, and indeed, of any cause. Their risk remained much less even considering other factors, such as weight, smoking habits, physical activity levels, calorie intake and alcohol consumption. The scientists noted, however, the lack of evidence for any direct link between low blood pressure and a lower risk of fatal cardiovascular disease, and concluded that cocoa has ingredients that promote the health of our circulatory system healthy in a variety of ways. For example, cocoa, a rich source of antioxidants, able to limit the tissue damage due to the extremely reactive chemicals called free radicals, which our body's energy-producing processes release, also has chemicals called flavan-3-oils, linked to lower blood pressure, and improved functioning of blood vessels' cell linings. Other scientists are cautioning the public on using the study as a license to gorge on cocoa products, emphasizing that there are much better ways of improving heart health. For example, Cathy Ross, medical spokesperson for the British Heart Foundation notes, "There is some evidence that when eaten in small quantities, dark chocolate might have some beneficial effects on blood vessels and lowering blood pressure, but as yet no study has investigated the long-terms clinical effects. This small study from Holland reinforces the fact that more still needs to be done to determine how eating cocoa affects coronary heart disease in the long term." She added that one would need to consume 100g of dark chocolate per day for the suggested therapeutic amount, which few would tolerate well anyway, or put differently, that one would not obtain the same effect consuming less than an average intake of 500 calories per 100g and an average 30% of fat. This is no doubt, the sort of evidence-based and balanced information the public should have that would be invaluable in decision-making regarding say whether or not to continue to guzzle dark or any other kind of chocolate in the hope of reducing one's risk of heart problems. Yet, there are many misinformed men and women out there or those who lack any information other than what they obtained from friends who themselves probably read about the health benefits of chocolates from a Web site owned by some chocolate marketer or enthusiast. The point here is that information technologies have a key role to play in disseminating health information but that such information needs to be credible, current, accurate and targeted, if it were not to be unhelpful, or worse still outright dangerous to health. Consider another recent research study published in the same issue of the journal mentioned earlier. Prostate diseases are relatively common in older men, although younger men also have them, including prostate cancer, for which many receive androgen deprivation therapy. This treatment has side effects such as depression, memory difficulties, and fatigue, termed the androgen deprivation syndrome. Researchers at the University of Texas Medical Branch, Galveston found the risks associated with androgen deprivation markedly less or nonexistent on adjustment for variables such as comorbidity, tumor characteristics, and ages. They concluded that depressive, cognitive, and constitutional disorders occur more commonly in patients receiving androgen deprivation, but this seems to be largely due to patients receiving androgen deprivation therapy being older, and having more comorbid illnesses, and more advanced cancers. Could this information not make a difference to treatment compliance among patients and in fact make it easier for the primary care physicians who follow up these patients to explain certain aspects of the treatment, including new and emergent symptoms, to the patients? Could such information not help reassure the patient and his relatives, improve compliance, satisfaction with care, and the patient's quality of life despite a having life-threatening illness? Could it not also help in treatment planning, for example, in decision-making regarding whether to prescribe other medications in the event that these adverse effects arise? In short, does this not also exemplify the value of accurate and targeted health information? The challenge therefore, is to develop software and other technologies to enable such targeted information provision. Could entrepreneurs or firms, health insurance firms, and software and ICT companies not collaborate to develop such software to which patients and physicians could subscribe that would provide them not just with medical news but current health information analyzed and tailored to the particular needs of the healthcare providers and their clients? Considering that, such information could help prevent illnesses, and reduce morbidities and mortalities there could be substantial savings in healthcare costs with such initiatives, which sh ould interest all keen on curtailing the increasing costs of health services provision.

M any people including men think that only women have breast cancer, but they are wrong. Men also have the condition. In fact, this misconception about breast cancer probably partly explains why men are dying pointlessly from the disease. Men are simply not aware that they could have it, or of the symptoms, or if they did, feel too embarrassed to seek medical help. About 250 men receive the diagnosis of breast cancer in the UK alone annually, 70 of them dying from the disease according to Guy's Hospital, Professor Ian Fentiman, in an article in the February 18, 2006 issue of the Lancet6. The expert noted that 50% of male patients do not receive the diagnosis until their cancer has advanced common signs for examples a painless lump in the chest or an inwardly turned nipple, totally ignored or missed, the average length of time it takes men who discover a lump to visit their GP, about 16 months. Professor Fentiman noted that such as lump could also be a sign of gynaecomastia, which might be harmless, hence the significance of family practitioners in particular, who are likely to be seen first by affected men, to be able to recognize the significance of such a lump and the n eed or otherwise for further investigations and which sorts. This would not only reduce unnecessary suffering from this condition, but its early and prompt treatment could improve its outcome, reduce hospitalizations rates and stays, and help reduce the healthcare costs overall, associated with the condition. According to the Professor, "If diagnosed early enough, a man with breast cancer has between 75% - 100% chance of making a full recovery, but this can drop to as low as 30% for men with very advanced disease." He adds, "The main concern is that it's just something about which most are totally ignorant. Men are just not thinking about it." This again highlights the value of health information reaching its target audience in a timely and efficient manner, hence the need for the urgent and effective deployment of current and emerging information technologies, and investment in R&D in developing novel ones that could facilitate the achievement of this objective. As Professor Fentiman also noted, "There is evident need for national protocols for both information and support for men diagnosed with breast cancer." There is currently information on male breast cancer on the Internet, for example on the website, CancerHelp UK, but it would be even more effective for men to receive such information, analyzed and interpreted in light of the most current scientific evidence direct on their cell phones, BlackBerrys, Palm Pilots, or Pocket PCs. , for examples, even prompted to read them. Delivered in a condensed, easy to read forms with options to read fuller versions on their PCs, or read out to them on their iPods, or via any other multimedia portal, it would unlikely surprise developers of such technologies to discover that many men would subscribe to their services. Men need to know what is normal or abnormal, and to inform their physicians about any unusual changes soonest, but they first need to know the symptoms and signs of male breast cancer. Technology-enabled targeted information is no doubt the most efficient and cost-effective means of giving them this knowledge, and saving the lives of many men. There is no reason why we should be stuck with merely providing information on the Internet. With advances in technology should come new ideas about how best to get vital health

147

information across to those that need them, otherwise such information will just pile up on idle Websites, stale and redundant, adding to the already stifling information glut, occupying precious virtual space, and gulping money that could be useful for other health projects. As noted earlier, WebMD's personalized health service offers health news and customized content and tools, which if it included the sort of analyzed and targeted health information described above would be even further value proposition that could offer competitive advantage, especially with the added capability of delivering the information rather than and in addition to the individual seeking it. These features are particularly important regarding men, who researches show seek help and use health services less frequently than women do. Men's help-seeking practices and health service use are multidimensional involving biological, psychological, and sociological considerations. Furthermore, health service providers seem poorly equipped to deal with men's health issues appropriately. There is a need for improved multidisciplinary collaboration among healthcare professionals, for ongoing researches into men's health. It is also important to encourage the development of novel healthcare ICT and its diffusion in order to ensure that the outcomes of these efforts reach the people that need them. Many men for example would like to know that Vitamin D could inhibit the spread of prostate cancer cells, particularly those that have the disease. According to a recent study by University of Rochester Medical Center scientists, it does so by limiting the activity of two specific enzymes, proteases called matrix metalloproteinase and cathepsin. According to Yi-Fen Lee, Ph.D., an assistant professor of Urology at the Medical Center, and her associates, Vitamin D also increases the level of counterpart enzymes that inhibit matrix metalloproteinase and cathepsin. These findings, published in the January 2006 issue of the Carcinogenesis[7], provide scientific evidence for the possible beneficial effects of vitamin D in the treatment to prostate cancer patients with high levels of the enzymes. In fact, research evidence increasingly has showed that vitamin D suppresses the progression of the cancer but had little effect on plasminogen activators, which also are important in the spread of prostate cancer. The researchers used 1, 25-hydroxylvitamin D3, the most potent and active form of vitamin D in the human

148

body. They noted that each person is unique and stressed the need to customize the therapy. They also cautioned that people should not take large amounts of vitamin D without medical advice and supervision, not least because such high doses have significant side effects such as increasing blood calcium levels and damaging the kidneys. The researchers are also studying the possible benefits of other vitamins, such as vitamin E, or even medications, that could increase vitamin D's anti-cancer properties without increasing its toxicity. According to Professor Lee, "The best way to get vitamin D is to drink milk, get modest exposure to the sun, and take a vitamin pill to enrich the vitamin D, which might prevent cancer." These examples no doubt underline the need for targeted healthcare information in men, as does a recent research published by Gough and Conner, of the Department of Psychology, University of Leeds, UK, in the January 2006 issue of the journal, Social Science and Medicines. The authors noted the dearth of research on the meanings men attach to food or to the links between food and health, yet a surfeit of information on men's health highlighting forms of masculinity, for example, risk-taking, and invulnerability, as a factor that negatively influences men's health practices. They set out to analyze qualitatively men's accounts of food and health using concepts relating to masculinity. Their findings on a dataset of 24 interviews with UK men from a range of age and social class groups show two principal barriers to healthy eating in men, namely, cynicism about government health messages and a rejection of healthy food due to poor taste and inability to satisfy. Could these findings not help with planning and resource utilization in health promotion efforts targeted at men? Do they not indicate how the masculine ideals of rationality, autonomy, and strength could influence men's health, albeit it even negatively and how this knowledge should constitute an important element of content development and design in targeted health promotion efforts? Could there not be need therefore for the use of sophisticated health information technologies to ensure the effective delivery of such health messages, again within the context of the recognized masculine ideals? Would the gains in improved health derivable from these seemingly petty considerations not far outweigh what some might consider the hassles involved in getting things right? Healthy living, part of which involves

149

eating right is a major thrust of preventive health education efforts in recent times. Is it not also important that men eat right, and would it not be necessary to ensure the removal of all obstacles in the way of their so doing? In an analysis of gender-specific health reporting in the Bodenseekreis, German researchers, Szagun and Preuss noted the over-representation of male seniors in the population with health problems with significant implications for healthcare planning, and for implementing appropriate prevention and intervention strategies, including risk avoidance measures and encouraging and boosting responsibility for health9. The authors also noted that in future, men's health and male-specific health reporting would become exceedingly important. In a gender-specific life table analysis for 1998 to 2002, they found higher average life expectancy in Baden-Württemberg and the Bodenseekreis compared to other regions in Germany, women generally living longer than men, in 2000, 82 years (Bodenseekreis: 82.2) in women, and 76.4 years (Bodenseekreis: 77.3) in men. The chief causes for the 5.6-year difference in life expectancy included cardiovascular diseases, cancers, road traffic accidents, and suicide. An analysis of death risks specific to age and gender revealed some potential health promotion and disease prevention approaches based on identification of critical phases of life, namely infancy, as evaluations of school enrolment differences revealed important variations in health problems; with early adulthood; and old age also proving to be important periods with regard men-specific health problems and interventions. The authors recommended targeted gender-specific health reporting, health promotion and prevention efforts aimed at men, who constitute a significant proportion of any human population, yet seems disadvantaged based on the life expectancy figures they found relative to women, which indeed, hold for many other countries. To be sure, the concept of targeted health information is not restricted to men, or for that matter, to women, or to any other groups. In fact, its underlying thrust is for the development and propagation of accurate and current health information content aimed at the people that need it the most and delivered via the most efficient and effective, ICT-based means, within the context of the most significant peculiarities of the targeted individuals in order to facilitate their receipt and utilization of the information. This concept means that it is not sufficient to create health information Web sites. Such health information would probably reach only an insignificant number of those that need it, the information lost in the maze of other such information that dot the World Wide Web. It is important in the current state of affairs, with a variety of sophisticated information technologies emerging, for critical health information to reach its target audience. How might this work? A firm develops or acquires the technology, perhaps some customized data mining technologies that could enable it gather, collate, and group research data and information in different health domains, and on different diseases and health, fitness, wellness and other health information. The company has trained and qualified staff to analyze the data and information and present the analysis in the right format and contextually as defined above, or acquires the necessary technologies to perform these functions. The company then sends out accurate and current information to subscribers via emails, cell phones, text messaging, mobiles devices, and a variety of other multimedia channels of the subscriber's choice, who receives an alert with the information delivered. Technology convergence will continue to provide immense opportunities for such information delivery, as for example, Vincent Cerf, widely deemed one of the "fathers of the Internet," notes, "Users will also begin using their mobile devices to control and manage other Internet-enabled appliances (medical, entertainment, and household equipments, among others.) Your mobile might become the moral equivalent of a remote control device that works anywhere in the world. You might activate a high-res display and vector video/audio/imagery/maps content by a few buttons pushes on a mobile keyboard." The company could acquire subscribers via a host of marketing outlets including Internet, radio, print, and TV commercials, and via alliances with health insurance firms, and healthcare providers. The most important thing is that subscribers are able to obtain information that they need promptly on the disease or subject to which they have subscribed. Only then could we be confident that we would achieve our goals for releasing health information to the public in the first place. Novel technologies aimed at bringing order to the prevailing information bedlam would certainly facilitate information targeting. One such technology is a new software system that enables speedier and more inclusive analysis of enormous quantities of information [10]. This software not only creates order out of information pandemonium and enables computers to perform tasks that only people could hitherto perform it could also create new information from old, its versatility demonstrated by real life scenarios. In one instance, a biotech industry market-consulting firm used the software to query situations-vacant advertising and business information newswires in order to forecast new drugs and products development by individual firms, which shows how it could create high value-added analyses from even data and information in the public domain. The Greek Ministry of Defence (MoD) also utilized the software to assemble pertinent information on terrorist groups from its own files and newspaper reports automatically. Unilever used it to analyze journal articles, newspaper reports, and other sources to create a composite of the association of weight, health, and food, much like putting together known knowledge of the natural history of diseases, including for example, their prevalence, causes, clinical presentation, treatment, and outcome. According to Dr Babis Theodoulidis, Senior Lecturer at the University of Manchester's Institute of Science, Technology, and coordinator of the IST-funded PARMENIDES project developing these tools, "Our greatest contribution was to create a framework for integrating structured and unstructured information". This no doubt is precisely what targeted information needs to sieve and structure the mostly unstructured text such as reports, articles, indeed, any information not part of a database, that most current information constitutes, automatically, an analysis that previously required human intervention, often with significant costs implications, particularly for very large and complex data as medical data and information. According to Dr. Theodoulidis, "Analyzing structured data is not new. Analyzing unstructured information using computers is only a recent development, but integrating and analyzing the combined data has never been done before. Our framework makes that possible." There is no doubt about the likely increasing use of this valuable software in the health industry, and indeed, in other industries. The PARMENIDES framework could perform cross-sectional and longitudinal analyses, enabling the system to identify new trends or developments that would otherwise be cryptic, for example, Healthcare consultant BioVista, to pool recruitment and business data and track the changing research priorities in biotech firms over time. Additionally, it could actually create new, unseen information from old data. Based on ontologies, with a vocabulary of all the significant words for a particular domain, such as healthcare, and the association between each word, which computers could then recognize contextually, this software, uses an ontology to analyze unstructured text, another, databases, and yet another to fuse the two by data sets. The scientists also developed tools to enable the semi-automatic creation of ontologies, making it possible to use them to create new ontologies, or to allow two unlike ontologies in the same domain, for example, healthcare, to exchange information automatically, and are developing the technology to work on a Grid-based architecture, which Theodoulidis described as its ideal milieu. There is no gainsaying the benefits of disease prevention, nor could one underestimate the health and pecuniary benefits of early diagnosis and treatment and of reducing the complications of diseases including via the establishment of appropriate rehabilitation programs. These primary, secondary, and tertiary prevention measures benefit immensely from the implementation of appropriate and effective healthcare ICT, such as that discussed above, and on ensuring that critical health information reaches the desired targets, the costs involved likely outweighed by the benefits of the technologies at least in the long term.

Healthcare ICT is helping to improve men's health in many ways. An important driver of the quest for information technologies to play an even greater role in men's health is the ever-rising costs of healthcare. In the US for example, spending forecasts include a rise of up to 20% of the country's gross domestic product (GDP) within a decade, reaching a total of $4 trillion, outpacing economic growth every year for the next ten years, increasing at an average annual rate of 7.2% per year during the same period. Health Affairs published these predictions by a number of experts in its Web exclusive online on February

22, 2006₁₁. The biggest recent increase was in 2002, when health spending increased by 9.1%. Expected rise in private health insurance within a decade is 6.6%. Many are convinced that these figures are unsustainable and would drive the US economy into even deeper recesses. Could the shift in emphasis to population health be responsible for home health spending being the fastest growing health-spending sector, as is currently the case? Would this trend if it persisted, healthcare ICT-backed, eventually result in a significant reduction in overall health spending in the US? Hospital spending would be double its current amount by 2015, reaching a high of $1.2 trillion dollars, according to the experts' forecasts. There could be a significant reduction in this figure if the current rend toward ambulatory and domiciliary healthcare continued. Many of the health problems that men for example have are preventable, with attitudinal changes that result in healthier lifestyles, including healthy food choices, and plenty of exercises. If the prevalence rates, morbidities, and mortalities, of chronic diseases such as cardiovascular diseases, and diabetes, fall because of these attitudinal changes, so would the need for hospitalization, and the amount spent on prescription drugs, expected to be about $446 billion in 2015, compared to $188 billion in 2004, growth for the next ten, estimated at 8.2% per year. This could translate into a healthier male population and significant curtailment of health spending over time. Would the ongoing investments in healthcare ICT that is facilitating these preventive efforts, and enabling the delivery of qualitative ambulatory and domiciliary health services, for example, electronic health records (EHR), electronic medical records (EMR), and telehealth, to name a few, not have been worthwhile? Medicare spending in the US in 2015 would be $792 billion according to these forecasts compared with $309 billion in 2004, and out of pocket payments,$421 billion during the same period, compared to $248 billion 2005. Would these figures not fall drastically with a healthier populace? Is it not therefore reasonable to conclude that healthcare ICT is playing a key role in healthcare delivery and would continue to do so in future? If this were so, why would it not be reasonable for healthcare providers to embrace information technologies even more and faster than currently in their practices? Would it not be necessary to explore the various barriers to healthcare ICT adoption by not only healthcare providers but also all healthcare stakeholders and take the necessary measures to remove these barriers considering all at stake doing otherwise? As mentioned earlier, even the public, justifiably skeptical of the security and privacy of health information moving from one provider to the next, and possibly other entities in the healthcare delivery chain, is changing its attitude toward health information technologies. The public is becoming increasingly confident of the technological and legislative measures in place and reviewed on an ongoing basis, and embracing these technologies. Why should healthcare providers, who should be leading the way in embracing them seemingly doing the opposite? Healthcare professionals have a variety of reasons for being slow in implementing these technologies, and we should be addressing their concerns as well, and encouraging them to invest in and implement healthcare ICT in their practices. Indeed, the Bush administration clearly had this in mind in the President's proposal during the last State of the Union speech regarding putting a cap on malpractice suits, but would adopting technology-backed, evidence-based practice for example, not in fact obviate the need for malpractice suits? In fact, is the current push toward consumer-driven care going to leave healthcare providers much choice regarding implementing healthcare ICT? How would a provider expect to be competitive not implementing cutting-edge information technologies that enhance the provider's value proposition, yet hope to attract an increasingly discerning clientele population? Health insurance firms, pharmacies, and other healthcare stakeholders including suppliers would also need to join the efforts to automate healthcare delivery, efforts bound to impact service provision to men and ultimately their health. For example, the Kaiser Family Foundation's Commission on Medicaid and the Uninsured reported the findings on February 28, 2006, of a 50-state survey of Medicaid officials it recently sponsored. The aim of the survey was to assess the early experiences of states regarding the shift of low-income seniors and people with disabilities enrolled in both Medicaid and Medicare (dual eligibles) to the Medicare Part D drug benefit. Health Management Associates conducted the survey, which explored the sort of problems the states have been experiencing during the transition, what they are doing to correct them, and ensure temporary coverage, and specific data on the costs of these temporary programs. On 1 January 2006, the prescription drug coverage for over 6 million US residents referred to as dual eligibles shifted from Medicaid into the new Medicare prescription drug benefit. It soon became clear to the Centers for Medicare and Medicaid Services at the Federal level and state and local officials that the transition was creating more difficulties for some dual eligibles to obtain needed prescriptions, many of these problems attributable to the legacy information systems coping poorly with the sudden surge in information traffic. Because dual eligibles usually have more wide-ranging health and prescription drug needs than other beneficiaries do, many states had anticipated problems with the transition and developed temporary programs to forestall them, reimbursement for which costs the federal government is offering. Medicaid officials from all 50 states and the District of Columbia participated in the survey, which showed that in the first month of implementation, more than 60% of states reported problems affecting a significant number of dual eligibles, resulting in 37 states implementing temporary coverage programs for them. The commonest problems were incorrect cost sharing charged to beneficiaries, in 49 states, pharmacies unable to bill plans, in 44 states, and beneficiaries unable to obtain non-formulary drugs, in 43 states. These are all technology-related problems that a variety of healthcare ICT, for examples precise, appropriate and sophisticated database, billing and pharmacy systems, adequate for the increased workload that the transition entails could help alleviate if not completely solve. Is it possible that these problems would have adversely affected the health of many poor, elderly or disabled men, and contrariwise saved others from possibly imminent death with their resolution, the states implementing the relevant information technologies? New information technologies continue to emerge that could help prevent these and other information management issue in the health system. Fraunhofer Institute for Integrated Circuits IIS in Erlangen manages the monitoring system *senSAVE*, which offers 24-hour telemedicine health care, for example. *senSAVE* is a radio networked monitoring system of intelligent sensors, integrated into a shirt for example, for wireless ECG data recording, additional sensors attached to the body to measure other vital medical parameters such as blood pressure and blood oxygen saturation. *SenSAVE* evaluates the patient's physical condition, recognizes its problems, if any, and alerts the doctor if an emergency arose, the alert via online connection to the medical practice, the hospital, or a medical service center, enabling the doctor to analyze critical information that could facilitate accurate diagnosis and treatment. *SenSAVE* is no doubt valuable for monitoring at home, individuals at risk for cardiovascular diseases, including the elderly, and those that already have these conditions, by a variety of healthcare providers such as doctors, and nurses, and the patients themselves, its miniaturized wireless sensors easy to attach, change, and to wear. Such ambulatory monitoring enhances the patients' quality of life (QOL) further enhanced with the patient having the opportunity to receive treatment in the comfort of his/her home, and among loved ones. E-prescribing is not just enhancing patient safety it is also improving generic medication use hence saving costs. Prescribing 500,000 medications using this approach, doctors at Michigan's Henry Ford Medical Group, involved in an e-prescribing project, did not just improve the use of generic medications by 7.3 percent, it saved $3.1 million in pharmacy costs in one year. Indeed, the Group now has 300 doctors at 24 medical centers per week using DrFirst's e-prescribing management technology. The doctors changed or cancelled over 50,000 prescriptions alerted to medications on the formulary, hence increasing the use of generic drugs and over 80,000 after drug-to-drug interaction alerts. E-prescribing is likely to gain increasing currency over time considering growing concerns over patient safety, and healthcare spending. The health industry will continue to benefit from progress in technology in future. According to Howard Schmidt, a former security expert with companies such as eBay and Microsoft, and is a former U.S. cybersecurity czar, "Everything, including coffee pots, home lighting, alarm systems, autos and heart pacemakers, will have a secure IP (Internet protocol) address and be able to be controlled by the owner. RFID (radio frequency identification tags) will know when you use up the last bag of corn, add it to your e-shopping list, and transmit it to the grocery store for you the next time you go shopping or if you elect to do home delivery." The use of RFID is also increasing in healthcare delivery to track medication use, hospital equipments shared by different units, and the elderly that have a tendency to wander away from their hospital beds, making it a key technology for ensuring patient safety, and optimizing resource utilization both, veritable cost saving measures. There is indeed, a variety of ICT life-saving devices for examples wearable alert systems that elderly or disabled males, or those living alone could use to call for help in case of a fall at home, and telemonitoring systems for ambulatory and domiciliary management of chronic and other illnesses. With regard security concerns, Schmidt said, "We will have self-healing, self-repairing and self-configuring computer systems that effectively "sandbox" programs so one can perform the function they want at the moment (or multitask) without exposing nonused functions," in a recent CNN interview.

The concept of targeted information mentioned earlier is not only for patients.

Physicians will also benefit from receiving important updates on medical knowledge, medications, procedures, and devices. The US National Institutes of Health for example is launching an all-inclusive program to educate doctors on the management of hypertension, which is likely to result in the wider use of low-priced diuretics12. The program will distribute the results of the antihypertensive and lipid lowering treatment to prevent heart attack trial (ALLHAT), which tested four classes of blood pressure lowering medications and found that inexpensive diuretics are as effective as newer, more expensive medications. The National Heart, Lung, and Blood Institute incorporated the ALLHAT results into clinical guidelines it issued in May 2003, the guidelines' main recommendation, that a low-cost diuretic be the first drug for most hypertensive patients on monotherapy, and one of the medications for patients on more that one medication. Healthcare ICT is no doubt going to play an important role in disseminating this information. With President Bush proposing to cut the Medicare budget by $36bn (£21bn; €30bn) over five years, such measures would certainly help alleviate concerns about health spending, particularly on prescription medications, a huge guzzler of healthcare resources, in the country.

The President also plans to achieve this goal by reducing the rate of increase in payments to healthcare providers and by increasing the premiums for people on higher incomes. Prior to now, all Medicare beneficiaries made the same monthly payments to cover doctors and outpatient services, $88.50 in 2006, but recent Medicare reforms proposing differentiated premiums based on income will start in 2007, increases the President's proposal, published on February 6, 2006, part of the White House budget, would speed up. The proposals would also reduce planned increases in payments to hospitals and to home health and skilled nursing facilities and would expand competitive bidding for lab services. These proposals no doubt underscore the determination of the Bush administration to reduce health spending, but they also reveal its interest in promoting competition in the health industry, itself intrinsically tied to consumer choices, in concert with other market forces. It is doubtful that anyone would contend the key role that information technologies would play in this scenario, and to emphasize the commitment to choice central to the consumer-driven healthcare model, officials of the UK National Health Service (NHS) information technology (IT) program, reassured the public in mid-February 2006 regarding upholding the policy on patients' consent. This policy allows patients that do not want their data on the new information systems shared to opt out, the NHS noting that the alternative "opt in" policy, which the General Practitioners Committee of the British Medical Association (BMA) proposed would compromise the quality of healthcare delivery. In response to fears about privacy and confidentiality regarding the decade long scheme to create a system of shared electronic health records (EHR) in the country, with central contracts worth over £6bn ($10.4bn; €8.7bn) the officials also assured the public of plans to make changes to the way the scheme's central systems deal with patient information on patients. It would indeed, be important for health information systems to ensure the security and privacy of patient information to secure increasing public confidence in them, a crucial requirement for individuals to opt in and for the realization in full of the numerous and immense benefits derivable from implementing these technologies both for men's health and for the health of all. Healthcare ICT has the potential to improve the quality of healthcare delivery and to reduce health costs simultaneously, concerns not restricted to governments but also employers, actions attributable to which latter employers recently took, for example massive worker layoffs, clearly indicative of these concerns, which have profound effects on the health of workers, in service, and retired. Indeed, a US federal judge on March 1, 2006 granted preliminary approval to Ford Motor Co.'s deal with the UAW to cut the firm's health care costs by instituting deductibles and monthly premiums for hourly retirees, a similar deal by GM in the offing. These deals on receipt of final approval mean that retired hourly workers would start paying monthly premiums, deductibles, and co-payments for medical services up to a maximum of $370 a year for individuals and $752 for a family, which they do not currently pay. The deals would affect about 150,000 Ford and 475,000 GM retirees and dependents. The U.S. District Judge Robert H. Cleland will hold a two-day hearing in a week, to hear objections to GM's deal to slash $1 billion a year from the firm's health care costs, a deal which over 1,240 retirees protest. However, GM insists that without reducing its $74 billion health care liability, its future is "at serious risk". In fact, GM is also reducing health care benefits for salaried retirees and restructuring its U.S. pension plan for them, planning to cap contributions for salaried retiree health care at 2006 levels beginning Jan. 1, 2007. These developments underscore the importance of all healthcare stakeholders instituting measures that would reduce healthcare spending by all payers, without compromising the quality of healthcare delivery, yet making health services affordable and accessible to all. Because healthcare information technologies could make the achievement of these objectives possible, the onus is on healthcare stakeholders to embrace these technologies. These technologies could also help with the issue of making consumers aware of medical prices, an important element of the consumer-driven healthcare model, regarding options to choose providers based on competitive pricing. As expected, this issue has been generating controversy among healthcare stakeholders, the president-elect of the American Medical Association Dr William Plested, on February 28, 2006 in the Wall Street Journal emphasizing that all payers and not just providers are involved in setting medical prices. The president-elect insists that payers also need to publicize their rates and that only then would consumers see the real fall in prices that they expect market forces to engender. Dr Plested also noted that "mega mergers" of insurance companies compel doctors "to sign up with the biggest health plan in town -- take it or leave it," leaving patients and doctors to "struggle" to determine what insurance would cover. Dr. Plested added, "If we want patients to become more prudent purchasers of health care, they need to be in greater control of their own health insurance choices and decisions and need price transparency from all sectors of the health care system." There ought to be ways by which the respective player in the healthcare scene could not only disclose pricing information, but also do so in ways that they reach those that need such information, in particular the consumers. Healthcare ICT could help in this regard, for example, facilitating access to such information on a dedicated Internet or other information dissemination portals. This would not only provide the required information to make choices regarding health services, it would inspire consumer confidence in the transparency of the health system, rectify market skew and improve its functioning, and enable the achievement of the desired objectives of consumer-driven healthcare delivery. The Internet as the preceding discussion shows is one of the most versatile information technologies applied to Medicine with even greater potential in future, and this much was evident at the recent 10th World Congress on the Internet in Medicine (WCIM - MedNet) held in Prague, Czech Republic between December 4 and 7, 2005. Knowledge acquisition and application in Medicine is undergoing remarkable transformation by ideas and technologies for examples telemedicine, unlimited database access, and open access medical literature[13]. Internet-based prescribing for example is gaining increasing currency in the US. The patient explores a menu of available drugs, makes a choice, and fills out a form to answer some medical questions and the doctor reviews the answers, and on approval writes and mails a prescription. The doctor may call the patient to clarify certain issues. Some have concerns about this approach including incomplete history, improper medical terminology, and there are of course, possibilities for litigation, making the future of this practice questionable. However, in a comparison of 2104 Internet patients seeking Viagra prescriptions online between June 14, 1998, and March 1, 1999, with regular practice, researchers found that doctors granted 2100 of 2104 requests, 310 requests, for medication refills, with no patient reporting any dissatisfaction [14]. The study also revealed no deaths or serious complications, nor any increase in the incidence of adverse effects. It also noted that Internet-obtained medical history was more complete, and the service was not solely for prescribing medications associated with sexual activity, lifestyle, or cosmetics, as some believe, and is safe, speedy, and cost and time effective, the consultation fee, a mere US $50, in some practices. The Internet has also offered opportunities for online counseling for some time now, for childhood obesity and bedwetting, for examples, conditions for which stigma and embarrassment may prevent children and adolescents from wanting to seek medical help. Some practitioners have reported significant success helping their patients with this treatment approach. Researchers have in fact shown evidence of the value of the sort of targeted information mentioned earlier. A Finnish scientist, Dr Doupi, developed the Structured Evaluated Personalized Patient Support (STEPPS), to improve access to patient information, including delivering personalized, customized patient education based on the integration of electronic patient record data and health information obtained online [15, 16]. The idea of STEPPS is to sieve information and choose for the individual, among online health information, the most relevant and reliable material. STEPPS also extracts relevant data from the electronic patient record automatically, using it to search Internet health information pages. It then selects the most relevant pages whose quality an expert team evaluates before sending the customized health information to the individual that requested it. As previously noted, this is clearly the direction patient health information ought to head, as it offers individuals the health information that they need rather the individual having to search for this information amidst the maze of information a customary Internet search would retrieve. This way, pertinent and reliable health information, and not a mass of stale and unreliable information, reaches the right target, making the information more valuable in disease prevention and treatment, and in health promotion, important aspects of any effort to improve population health, and to save healthcare costs. To underscore the concern for the quality and reliability of health information on the Internet, attributes no doubt difficult to ensure and control, an Internet Corporation for Assigned Names and Numbers (ICANN) study group once proposed the establishment and licensing of top-level domains (TLDs),World Health Organization-sponsored, in the form "dot.health" (.health), to no avail. Other initiatives exist for examples, the Health on the Net (HON) Code of Conduct, and the European Project Worldwide Online Reliable Advice to Patients and Individuals (WRAPIN,) all still struggling with the issue. There is therefore, some believe an urgent need for an effective central organization that would ensure the reliability of online health information, the bias and inaccuracy characteristic of some content indeed, a potential health hazard. Such an organization would complement and in fact reinforce present efforts such as consumer awareness and education, Internet health data providers' self-censorship, and inclusive third party and peer-review appraisals.

Recent experiences with drugs prices for some of the most popular medicines

seniors use hiking an average of 4% since the introduction of the new Medicare drug benefit plan in the US suggests that the publicizing prices on the Internet for example, is one thing, patients paying those prices, another. The Democratic staff of the House of Representatives Government Reform Committee released a report on February 21, 2006, which examined plans that Aetna Inc., Humana Inc., Medco Health Solutions Inc., and AARP/UnitedHealth Group Inc. offer. The report stated that prices for Pfizer Inc.'s pain reliever Celebrex, Merck Inc.'s cholesterol drug Zocor and eight other top drugs 10 major plans offer increased during the program's first seven weeks, in some cases by as much as 10%. With the voluntary program, Medicare's elderly and disabled beneficiaries ought to be able to choose from a host of plans health insurers and others administering health care plans called pharmacy benefit managers offer. Further, participants pay a part of their drug costs and monthly fees, the latter waived for low-income earners. However, states the report, "The private insurers offering the new Medicare drug plans are not providing seniors and individuals with disabilities with low drug prices,"'"..the rise outpaced inflation as well as drug price increases

163

found via drugstore.com and in Canada." These developments seem to be counter to the goals of consumer-driven healthcare of giving consumers options and lowering prices, many would argue, and justifiably so, although Medicare officials insist that this is a temporary setback due to rising wholesale prices and other factors, rather than a response to the new Medicare program. The Pharmaceutical Care Management Association, which represents pharmacy benefit managers also flawed the report for excluding generic drugs and those obtainable via mail order, which some plans offer. The association also noted its ongoing negotiations for lower prices with drug manufacturers and that, prices under the Medicare plan were actually lower by 35% earlier in February than retail, but this report found that only Avantra's RX Premier plan of the 10 surveyed, reduced its prices, by an average of 1.1%. Indeed, a second report the same committee released found current prices plans offer higher than with Medicare s temporary drug cards in the past two years. Although it is possible for patients to swap plans once a year, companies have no limits on how frequently they change prices. Some observers are speculating that these developments would affect substantially, enrollment for the government's new program, for which the Bush administration aims to get Medicare's 42 million beneficiaries to sign up, although only 3.6 million have done so voluntarily to date, another 20 million, enrolled automatically from other programs. These issues also reflect the intricate operations and imperfections of the market, and the impact they could have on men's health, and of course on the health of everyone else. They also point to the need for more information on the workings of such government programs, for example on choice of medications, generics much cheaper than brands for example. However, it takes some time for information to reach its audience especially if not targeted, in this case to seniors and people with disabilities, some of whom may currently lack crucial information on making the sort of choices consumer-driven healthcare presumes they would. We need to step up efforts to promote healthcare ICT diffusion across board, not just among healthcare providers, but all healthcare stakeholders. Considering that much is at stake, as the above example, with likely information asymmetry threatening to create the impression that an almost-certainly well meaning government program is having the exact opposite effect shows, not to mention the immense benefits of information technologies on individual health, and the opportunities they provide for curtailing health spending it is time indeed we did.

References

1. Available at: http://www.ustreas.gov/offices/public-affairs/hsa/pdf/hsa-basics.pdf
Accessed on February 27, 2006

2. Available at: http://www.insureusa.org/news/press17.htm
Accessed on February 27, 2006

3. Available at:

http://www.medicalnewstoday.com/medicalnews.php?newsid=36917
Accessed on February 27, 2006

4. Buijsse B, Feskens EJM, Kok FJ, & Kromhout D. Cocoa Intake, Blood Pressure, and Cardiovascular Mortality: The Zutphen Elderly Study. *Arch Intern Med*. 2006; 166:411-417.

5. Shahinian VB, Kuo Yong-Fang, Freeman JL, and Goodwin JS. Risk of the "Androgen Deprivation Syndrome" in Men Receiving Androgen Deprivation for Prostate Cancer. *Arch Intern Med*. 2006; 166:465-471.

6. Fentiman IS, Fourquet A, Hortobagyi GN. *The Lancet* - Vol. 367, Issue 9510, 18 February 2006, Pages 595-604

7. Bo-Ying Bao, Shauh-Der Yeh, and Yi-Fen Lee 1, 25-dihydroxyvitamin D3 inhibits prostate cancer cell invasion via modulation of selective proteases *Carcinogenesis* Advance Access published on June 29, 2005 *Carcinogenesis* 2006 27: 32-42; doi:10.1093/carcin/bgi170

8. Gough B, and Conner MT Barriers to healthy eating amongst men: a qualitative analysis *Soc Sci Med* 2006 Jan; Vol. 62 (2), pp. 387-95.

166

9. Szagun B & Preuss S. Gender-specific health reporting in the Bodenseekreis: future theme of "health in boys and men" Gesundheitswesen (Bundesverband Der Ärzte Des Öffentlichen Gesundheitsdienstes (Germany)) [Gesundheitswesen] 2005 Dec; Vol. 67 (12), pp. 862-8.

10. Available at:

http://istresults.cordis.lu/popup.cfm?section=news&tpl=article&ID=80902&AutoPrint=True
Accessed on March 1, 2006

11. Borger C, Smith S, Truffer C, Keehan S, Sisko A, Poisal J, and Kent Clemens M. Health Spending Projections through 2015: Changes on the horizon. *Health Affairs* 25 (2006): w61-w73

12. Available at:

http://bmj.bmjjournals.com/cgi/content/extract/332/7538/379-a
Accessed on March 1, 2006

13. Goran MJ, Stanford J. E-health: restructuring care delivery in the Internet age. *J Healthc Inf Manag.* 2001; 15:3-12

14. Jones MJ, Thomasson WA. Establishing guidelines for Internet-based prescribing. *South Med J.* 2003;96:1-5

15. Doupi P, van der Lei J. Towards personalized Internet health information: the STEPPS architecture. *Med Inform Internet Med.* 2002;27:139-151. Abstract

16. Doupi P, van der Lei J. Design and implementation considerations for a personalized patient education system in burn care. *Int J Med Inform.* 2005; 74:151-157.

The Future of Consumer Healthcare ICT

The pervasiveness of information and communications technologies (ICT) in contemporary times is not restricted to embedded software in virtually every item in household, office, and other gadgets. Indeed, ICT also plays a major role in healthcare delivery. Just as software embedded in our wristwatches, refrigerators, cookers, cars and trucks are crucial to their effective functioning, so are they in many devices doctors use in treating their patients, in many cases, their efficient operations key to successful treatment, if not the survival of the patient. However, ICT is not only important in the health sector for treatment purposes. It is also important in disease prevention, and in the rehabilitation of patients recovering from a variety of illnesses. It is also an important tool in health promotion. ICT finds institutional uses in all these different ways. Government agencies use ICT as an epidemiological and statistical instrument, in information gathering, collation, analysis, and sharing. With ICT, they are able to transform data into information and the latter into actionable knowledge that could help in preventing and responding effectively to outbreaks of communicable diseases such SARS and Avian influenza. ICT helps with governments' health education efforts to disseminate information on wellness, healthy living, and disease prevention, including health alert management, and vaccine inventory and immunization management. It helps them in analyzing health indicators crucial for health reform and policy formulation. Hospitals implement electronic health records (EHR) to streamline documentation management and facilitate real-time sharing and availability of patient information at the point of care (POC). They use radio frequency identification (RFID) chips, tiny microchips, smaller than a grain of sand, with antennae on them, to transmit a unique code or other data to an RFID reader without touching it, via radio transmission. These chips enable hospitals to automate certain processes and repetitive tasks and to provide safer, more efficient care to patients, cut costs, and to offer patients more information about their treatment. With RFID, hospitals no longer have to worry about where to find instruments that different units share or even those elderly patients that tend to wander away from their beds and hospital wards. Automated physician practices find it easier to schedule patient appointments or ensure correct billing, avoiding annoying and costly claims denials. Yet, healthcare ICT is not just for institutional use. There are many ICT applications individuals would find useful, sometimes even life saving in matters pertaining to their health, outside those their physicians, nurses, and other healthcare professionals use to treat them in hospitals and doctors' offices. What is more, with knowledge of the functioning of the human body in health and in disease ever improving, the opportunities for employing healthcare ICT by the individual to help in the achievement of his or her health goals seem limitless. Indeed, the healthcare industry is facing increasingly fewer options than to include consumers in the framework of contemporary healthcare degree, empowering them to participate in their healthcare, including making informed choices on matters pertaining to their health. Just considering the various ways ICT could help achieve these goals is sufficient to appreciate the current applications and enormous potential of healthcare ICT also for the individual. One could view health from several service perspectives. Let us start with one public health perspective that differentiates between primary, secondary and tertiary prevention. Primary prevention comprises interventions that prevent or delay the development of a disease. Secondary and tertiary prevention are interventions that focus on persons that suffer from a disease and seek, with the former, to prevent via early diagnosis, and prompt and effective treatment, or with the latter, to control, via appropriate rehabilitation services, the complications of the disease. What roles could ICT play in successfully implementing these interventions at the individual level? Could ICT help someone prevent a disease or delay its onset, or help someone who already has the disease prevent or control its complications? We will illustrate the answers to these questions with the natural history of some diseases to highlight not only that ICT already exists that is helping solve a variety of health problems, but also the immense opportunities for developing newer and even more sophisticated

169

ones. This is in keeping with the concept of first identifying the health problems to develop the technology to solve rather than the other way round. Before we do that though, let us see where technology is at with regard the health of the individual consumer considering a few examples.

Mothers can now rest assured that the lives of their newborn babies are no

longer at risk from sudden deaths. This is because there is now a wearable Motherboard Smart Shirt-T-shirt to track and record the vital signs wirelessly. This device could potentially save the lives of millions of infants. A significant proportion of the 3.8 million infants born annually are premature, suffer from apnea, are at risk of Sudden Infant Death Syndrome (SIDS), or have illnesses for example influenza or respiratory synctial virus, and require monitoring. For the over 500,000 infants in question, the use of an apnea monitor offers their parents some peace of mind. However, it still presents obtrusive discomforts, such as loose wires and high false alarm rates. The Wearable Motherboard Smart Shirt enables comfortable vital signs monitoring from virtually anywhere. Salient to the development of the platform is the integration of wireless technologies with wireless Local Area Network based on the IEEE 802.11 protocol and the wide area network used by third-generation broadband wireless. With the addition of a proprietary Applications Programming Interface (API), the dual platform technology acts as an open standard upon which existing medical monitoring firms can port their applications. The system's wireless platform uses the most appropriate communications protocol for a particular setting to transmit vital signs data non-stop, to a remote monitoring location staffed with trained technicians and physicians. Adverse vital signs indicating a potential medical event can trigger a rapid response by the health-monitoring unit, which would, no doubt help save lives. Regardless of who is using it-an infant or parent, a pregnant woman, or an elderly with cardiac symptoms, the Smart Shirt offers newfound security by enabling these individuals to go about their daily business with little awareness that they are under continuous and reliable monitoring.

The US Food and Drug Administration in 2004 approved an implantable computer chip through which a doctor could access his or her patients' health records. Developed by VeriChips, these microchips use radio frequency identification technology (RFID). This is the first time the FDA has approved the use of the device, used prior to now to track bird migration and merchandise in stores, whose serial number pulls up patients' allergies, medication history, blood type and other medical information. Doctors insert the chip under the patient's skin almost painlessly using a syringe. The process does not usually last longer than a quarter hour, and requires no suturing. As a scanner passes over the chip, it releases patient-specific information stored in its code, which the doctor can use at the point of care in patient management. Most people would agree that knowing the patient's allergies, past medications that worked for the patient's condition and other valuable will improve the quality of service delivery, at the point of care (POC), making the market opportunities of this and similar products potentially huge.

Falls among the elderly is a major health concern in an increasingly aging population such as in the industrialized world. Indeed, research studies show that 30% of persons over 65 years old fall every year, sometimes with serious consequences, and as many as 50% fall in 80s age range. It is bad enough that seniors often fall, but it could be fatal if no one was there to help. Falls are a major cause of physical injuries but they also cause a sometimes-debilitating fear of falling, loss of confidence, and self or caregiver-imposed restriction in mobility. Seniors may soon be able to venture outside their homes with greater confidence and independence, using the invention of Dr Francis Eng Hock Tay, an associate professor in the department of mechanical engineering at the national University of Singapore. This invention, termed Memswear because it uses MEMS (Micro-Electric Mechanical Systems) engineering, is a potentially life-saving jacket, shirt, or blouse that can call for help when its wearer falls. Current commercially available systems require a patient or a senior to wear an alarm device, which he or she will press in an emergency to seek help through telephone networks. With Dr Tay's device, the alarm will go off on its own and send a message to a predetermined person even if the wearer lost consciousness, or could not press the alarm for other reasons such as disorientation. There no doubt that this new gadget will reduce the time it takes help to arrive, and minimize the physical and psychological consequences of the fall. The sensor-transmitted device attached to a shirt, blouse, or jacket, uses Bluetooth technology. The 2cm by 2cm device detects the speed and tilt of the wearer and triggers a tiny transmitter affixed to the bottom of the garment if he or she fell. It sends the alarm to the wearer's home computer or cell phone, which in turn alerts a family member, friend, doctor, or caregiver. The team wants to make the device affordable and not more than $80 apiece. Buyers will also have the option of purchasing a waterproof version although they are now only removable sensors that one should not launder. Dr Tay and his team are working on advanced devices that can preempt falls, warning the wearer of an imminent fall, by beeping or some other means. Considering that not only is the developed world aging, the recent prediction of an international group of experts based on an examination of a systematic review of published studies on dementia that they received from the Alzheimer's Diseases International, a London-based organization, is ominous. This report, published in the December 17, 2005 issue of The Lancet, suggests that with 4.6 new cases of dementia yearly, the prevalence of the condition will double every two decades from its current estimated 24.3 million sufferers to 8.1 million in2040. The experts also noted that the doubling of prevalence rates would occur in developed countries such as the United States, but the rates would actually triple in China, India, and other countries in south Asia and the western Pacific. Experts are justifiably concerned that at these rates, Alzheimer's disease and other dementias are soon going to be major public health issues that would threaten the health and quality of life of many individuals and their families, and may significantly strain health systems, with potentially serious micro-and macro-economic consequences for many countries. What role could health ICT play in helping to reduce the risk factors for cerebral blood vessel damage, for examples, high blood pressure, smoking, diabetes, and cholesterol, which could help prevent this looming epidemic? What are the potential market opportunities for software and ICT companies that might outweigh the concerns of some for recouping the R&D funds they may need to invest in developing innovative technologies that could help solve problems relating to aging and dementia, or indeed, any other concerns that they may have regarding these health issues?

The Internet has proven to be a veritable information resource for everyone,

particularly with the increasing speed of Internet access, and the remarkable progress in broadband and akin technologies, and the public, exploiting today's widespread connectivity is increasingly using the Internet to seek health information. Indeed, a recent study published in the December 12/26 2005 issue of the Archives of Internal Medicine1, showed that individuals in the US are likely to first turn to the World Wide Web when seeking health information. However, they trust their physicians more to provide them with accurate medical information. The researchers noted the changing context in which patients consume health information with more people using the Internet, progress in telemedicine, and changes in media health coverage. The researchers, led by Dr. Bradford Hesse of the National Cancer Institute in Bethesda, Maryland, analyzed data obtained in the telephone-based, first Health Information National Trends Survey (HINTS) with 6369 adults interviewed between October 2002 and April 2003. Of the 63.0% of respondents that had used the Internet, 63.7% had sought some type of health or medical information. Less than 10% of users had engaged in other health-related Internet activities, such as purchasing medication, communicating with physicians, or participating in an online support group.

62.4% of respondents reported trusting their physicians "a lot" for cancer information, compared with 23.9% for the Internet. 49.5% would prefer to go first to their physicians for information about cancer, 49.5% reported wanting to go to their physicians, but in fact, only 10.9% of those who had sought information about cancer reported having sought information on cancer first from their physicians, compared to 48.6% that went to the Internet first. The evolution of the use of the Internet in healthcare is ongoing, and as individuals become more knowledgeable about health issues, the greater would likely be their demand for more active participation in their healthcare. This would require the development of more interactive Internet technologies, and of related technologies that would guarantee information security, privacy, and confidentiality. Such interactive technologies could package say specialty-specific health information that patients could access, which being necessarily accurate and current, as any serious-minded, image-conscious, healthcare provider would likely ensure, would save individuals exposure to inaccurate, even false health information that many websites allegedly unabashedly provide. Is it likely that some software firm is already looking at developing appropriate technologies to solve these problems? Governments could also help with regard the packaging of health information and ensuring that it is accurate and current as is that of New Jersey in the US, whose recently launched New Jersey HealthLink saves consumers the trouble of searching for health information at websites with questionable integrity dishing out information of equally suspect validity. New Jersey consumers will also not need to use Internet search engines or various state Web sites to learn about existing health care services, information that New Jersey HealthLink provides, made possible by the collaboration of five state departments, at Acting Gov. Codey's behest. The Web site aims to improve access to health care information creating opportunities for consumers to be actively involved in their healthcare by making it easier for them to take more-informed decisions regarding all aspects of their treatment. The Web site, which carries forward the success of the New Jersey Health Care Profile Web site, started in 2004 that gives information about physicians' backgrounds, has a number of helpful links, including among others, treatment/screening services, mental health, addiction, long-term care, insurance and financial assistance. It has over a hundred health-related services listed from A to Z, and orders information by user-groups, for examples children, families, the elderly, persons with disabilities, the uninsured, or not adequately insured.

Besides information, the Internet is also providing consumers, avenues for

purchasing medications, vitamins and a variety nutritional supplement, and other healthcare products. However, there have been concerns about these e-health transactions, the safety and efficacy of some of the products doubtful, and because the transactions are, in general, unregulated, many unscrupulous businesses getting away with unmitigated fraud. However, governments are starting to wade in more forcefully via regulations valid at least within their borders, surveillance activities, and other measures. In a release on December 23, 2005, Health Canada for example warned Canadians to be wary of buying Tamiflu online and to avoid anything called "generic Tamiflu" because generic versions of the anti-viral drug simply do not exist. Tamiflu, until recent reports of resistance to it due to mutation of the virus emerged in the New England Journal of Medicine, the day prior to the Health Canada release, was in the forefront in the fight against avian or bird flu. Health Canada released the warning after reports from the UK that many websites, two of them, Canadian, have been selling illegal Tamiflu to people in the UK, and other reports that the U.S. Customs Border Patrol intercepted over 50 shipments of bogus Tamiflu at their border. However, Health Canada reassured that there is no evidence of the presence of counterfeit Tamiflu in Canada, although could not rule out the chances otherwise, advising Canadians to buy Tamiflu with a prescription from a doctor and at a pharmacy known to them. Considering that the H5N1 virus has killed 71 persons in Asia since 2004, and there have been 139 affected individuals, 95 in 2005 alone according to the World Health Organization (WHO), Health Canada's concerns are no doubt justified. Individuals also correspond with their doctors by email, and text messages, to discuss treatment options, schedule, or cancel appointments, report medication side effects, or just seek advice on health-related issues. Many individuals are in fact already videoconferencing with their doctors, engaging in face-to-face communication via computers connected to the Internet. The individual simply sits in front of a Web camera, and speaks into a microphone. Data compression, then transmission ensues, straight to the doctor, who receives and views the data on video on a computer screen and listens to the audio via the speakers. However, these Internet modes of consultations raise important billing, and in some jurisdictions, even ethical and legal issues. There is also currently a variety of on-line screening devices individuals could use for anxiety disorders, mood disorders, and substance abuse disorders that are potentially valuable for clinical practice, and in some cases, for example, depression, possibly life saving. Other such online assessment tools could help screen for dementia, alcoholism, and other disorders. Some studies have shown that self-help treatment programs on stand-alone computers are just as effective as routine clinical care. The Internet therefore offers individuals prevention and therapeutic options right at home on their PC, including interactive doctor-patient encounters as previously noted, more customized treatments, and faster feedback on therapies. Indeed, randomized clinical trials (RCTs) have shown that Internet-based treatment is more effective than no-treatment at all and as effective as in-person treatment, although these researches had focused on anxiety disorders, burnout, depression, headache, insomnia, tinnitus, and obesity. Other researchers have shown that exposure through virtual reality is effective in a number of RCTs in specific phobias, although not conclusively so for other psychiatric disorders. These studies will likely stimulate more R&D interest in computer-driven and Web-based assessment and treatment considering the ever-increasing usage of the Internet worldwide[2].

Siemens Communications Inc., The Mount Sinai Medical Center, and

Elmhurst Hospital Center on December 13, 2005 announced an alliance to create patient smart card deployment, in New York City, that would help make important health care information more accurate, more secure, and more readily accessible. The Patient Health Smart Card initiative continues where the successful smart card pilot launched at Elmhurst Hospital in 2003, the first in New York, left off. This alliance, which is ongoing and includes developing other smart card technologies integrated with clinical and other information systems, aims to expand smart card technology in the metropolitan area, and create a regional health network. Planned for rollout in phases, participating healthcare institutions will issue their patients photo identification cards with embedded chips (smart cards) capable of storing patient information, which healthcare professionals involved in the regional smartcard network will update routinely. Patients will own the smart cards, loadable with patient information including demographics, medical histories, allergies, chronic diseases, current medications, drug interactions, adverse drug events, and laboratory results, among others, crucial to patient management at the point of care (POC.) Furthermore, the technology enables patients to have direct control of key medical data on a highly portable, secure platform, which is of immense benefits in our very mobile world, facilitating healthcare provision when needed, even far away from home. Besides making patient information available readily at the point of care (POC), the future of smart card technologies in healthcare is also promising if indeed, its strong authentication, secure networks and identity management technologies proved capable of protecting patient information and communication in the long term. Furthermore, by facilitating access to vital patient information when needed, the credit card-looking, chip-embedded smart cards also help to reduce medical errors caused by inaccurate, deficient, or even unavailable patient information; facilitate sharing of patient information among healthcare providers and; reduce wait times. The patient simply has to insert the card into a reader and enter his or her private Personal Identification Number (PIN) to unlock the card. This gives the health care facility instant access to the information on the card. The technology promises more cost-effective and secure movement of patient records between healthcare providers. However, it would only benefit individuals that use the services of participating healthcare providers with the sort of restricted deployment by the alliance mentioned above, hence the need for its widespread adoption in order for many more people to benefit from this useful technology.

I ncidentally, costs are major reasons slowing down the nationwide deployment

of electronic health records in many countries, even in the developed ones. This is understandable considering the sometimes-staggering costs of such an enterprise. According to a study by Richard Hillestad and his team at RAND3, published in the September/October 2005 edition of Health Affairs, it would take 15 years to implement a nationwide electronic health records network and cost hospitals about $98 billion and physicians about $17 billion. The study also noted that the average annual cost to hospitals would be $6.5 billion, and to physicians, $1.1 billion, but that if 90% of providers adopted EMR implementation and networking, annual saving would be $81 billion, including $77 billion from increased efficiency and $4 billion from decreased medical errors. This is not to mention the projected 200,000 yearly reduction in adverse drug events in inpatient hospital settings, and by two million in ambulatory settings, with annual cost savings of $1 and $3.5 billion in these settings respectively. The about 60% of savings to hospitals, expected from reduced adverse drug events in patients ages 65 and older, 40% to ambulatory practices, from decreased medication errors in the same age group are no doubt also substantial. The study, which also observed that only 20-25% of US hospitals and 15-20% of physician offices have implemented EHR and EMR systems, respectively, stressed that health ICT-enabled prevention and management of chronic diseases could eventually double those savings simultaneously increasing health and other communal benefits. It also emphasized that a national EHR network would save Medicare about $23 billion and private insurers about $31 billion annually, and that these savings would only materialize coupled with related modifications to the health care system, for example, if healthcare providers followed all checkup reminders and other prompts from the system. The findings in this study provide ample justification for governments to invest even if incrementally in the EHR infrastructures that would facilitate the adoption of EMR technologies by healthcare providers, which in turn would facilitate the widespread diffusion of such other valuable technologies as the Patient Health Smart Card among the public. One may ask what small and group practices benefit from investing in EMR technologies. Robert Miller and his colleagues at the University of California-San Francisco recently carried out case studies of fourteen solo or small-group primary care practices using EMR software from two vendors4. They found initial EMR implementation costs to average $44,000 per full-time equivalent (FTE) provider, ongoing costs, an average of $8,500 per provider annually. The researchers also noted that the average practice recouped its EMR costs in 2.5 years, although for some, much longer. With regard to group practices, a nationwide survey conducted by researchers at the Medical Group Management Association Center for Research and the University Of Minnesota School Of Public Health, and funded by the Agency for Healthcare Research and Quality, found that about 14.1% of group practices use an EMR system 5. The researchers also reported that the larger the size of the practice the higher the likelihood that they would have EMR systems. Thus, about 12.5% of practices with five or less full-time equivalent physicians had an EMR system, whereas 15.2% of practices with six to 10 FTE physicians, 18.9% for practices with 11 to 20 FTE physicians, and 19.5% for groups with 20 or more FTE physicians, did. The cost of the EMR system on the average was $32,606 per FTE physician, to buy and implement, and $1,500 per FTE physician to maintain it every month. There is no doubt about the need to formulate policies that offer inducements and support to encourage practices to implement EMR, which would no doubt improve the quality of the care that they deliver. Clearly, software and other ICT firms have much business considerations at stake in encouraging, even in promoting all the necessary facets of this process, whose outcome would be of immense benefits to individuals and to society. Incidentally, there seems to be changing public attitude towards EHR as a recent survey conducted in the US in March 2005 by Accenture revealed. Ninety three percent of respondents felt that EHR could improve the quality of care, 92% that it could reduce treatment error rates, and 75%, that it could reduce total healthcare costs. Sixty one percent of respondents were willing to pay monthly premiums for the EHR services used to manage their electronic health records, 55% affirming that such records are more secure than paper-based record systems, and 54% actually concerned about the safety and security of the latter. These findings indicate that the public is increasingly cognizant of the value of EHR, and should inspire physicians and health plans to implement it, as there is a higher likelihood that they would recoup their investments while at the same time improve the quality of their healthcare services. It should also encourage governments to invest more in EHR infrastructure. Indeed, a recent report by the US National Academy of Engineering and the Institute of Medicine titled, "Building a Better Delivery System: A New Engineering Healthcare Partnership" noting that the "collective inattention" to health information technology by the healthcare industry costs a half trillion dollars yearly in lost efficiency, suggests that it is in their best interests to do so. The report, which also noted that the healthcare industry, unlike other industries that have exploited engineering strategies and technologies to optimize performance and productivity, not so doing, has led in part to almost 100,000 annual preventable deaths, outmoded procedures by contemporary engineering standards, soaring healthcare costs at about thrice the inflation rate, and 43 uninsured Americans. Is it not time the healthcare industry got serious about health ICT, including embracing systems engineering tools that improved product safety and quality at reduced production costs, in other industries? Is the health industry not keen to implement the "six quality aims" that the Institute of Medicine recommended in its report "Crossing the Quality Chasm" of delivering safe, timely, efficient, equitable, and patient-centered "to the public, which adopting such engineering technologies would help achieve? The example of the cell phone below shows the cutting-edge functionalities that the health industry could derive from embracing advanced engineering technologies.

The cell phone is proving to be a versatile harbinger of healthcare ICT that

individuals are likely to find useful and to embrace in large numbers in the near future, thus far, courtesy of the pioneering efforts of a LG Electronics Inc., which has been in the top-five bracket of mobile phone manufacturers since 2004. The company earned this high industry ranking due largely to its commitment to developing innovative and cutting-edge mobile phone features and designs. Among its variety of new and innovative products are mobile phones that incorporate hi-fi technologies such as 5-megapixel digital cameras, 3D games, and Video-On-Demand (VOD), MP3 playback, video replay, voice recognition, satellite, Digital Multimedia Broadcasting (DMB), navigation and Personal Digital Assistant (PDA) functions, giving a new meaning to the phrase, "multifunctional digital convergence". LG Electronics has also developed health-related multimedia functions for its cell phones such as the blood

alcohol detector, introduced in 2005. It has also developed those capable of measuring blood sugar levels, body fat percentages, and stress levels. Could this be one solution to help individuals with a drinking problem know when to stop drinking, and when not to drive after having been drinking? Would this not help with drinking-related issues and problems such as road traffic accidents (RTA) and the needless deaths they cause on our roads? Does it take complicated math to figure the extent of the market for such ICT? How could the ability of individuals with diabetes to monitor their blood sugar on their cell phones help them to better manage their conditions, prevent complication s, and to reduce the incidence of negative outcomes? How useful would such a device be that could help detect diabetes, particularly the type 2 variant, before it ravages the body, considering its characteristic latency? How many people might want to purchase such a device even solely on being able to detect pre-diabetes? How much would that save in morbidity, and mortality, and in economic and other costs to society? How many more health indices could such innovative technologies detect, and what could an enterprising software/ICT firm lose developing products that could help individuals prevent diseases such as diabetes, reduce its complications, and enhance their quality of life?

The future of healthcare ICT for the individual consumer, as for health ICT in general, depends largely on the recognition by relevant stakeholders of the need to first identify a problem or process, and then develop the appropriate technologies to solve the problem or improve the process; not first build a "solution", and then grope around for problems to solve. There are different approaches to identifying health problems and processes with which ICT could help, but regardless of the approach adopted, the exercise would entail a thorough appraisal of medical knowledge and progress. One could focus on the health problems in the different age groups of the human developmental life cycle, for example. One could simply be interested in the health problems peculiar to the male or female sex. One might want to examine problems in different healthcare settings, for example, nursing homes. It is also possible to keep strictly within medical and surgical specialties, taking an in-depth look at the workflow of different specialists to see what ICT could help improve, or at disorders represented in these specialists, and the role ICT could play in improving their prevention and treatment. As previously noted, a public health approach would be to consider the primary, secondary, and tertiary interventions that ICT could facilitate regarding a particular health problem. The technologies developed using any of these approaches, would of course be contextual, regarding a health institution, state or provincial governments, or even an entire country, with whose business and long-term goals the technology goal ought to align. Let us examine the public health approach a little closer. Diabetes comprises a group of chronic diseases caused by inherited and/or acquired deficiency in the production of insulin by the pancreas, or by the resistance to the insulin produced. Either way, there is a consequent increased concentration of glucose in the blood, which over time damages many of the body's systems, particularly the blood vessels and nerves. Types 1 and 2 diabetes present with similar symptoms and signs although generally believed to have different origins, the former, inherited, the latter, acquired, in the main. World Health Organization (WHO) statistics reveal that an epidemic of diabetes is imminent in many parts of the world. In 1985, its worldwide prevalence was 30million. By 2000, it had become 177million, and continues to rise, estimated to increase by 160% by 2025, and to be 370 million in 2030 [6]. Diabetes affects 17 million or 6.2% Americans[7] 7.4% Australians[8], and according to 1996/97 Canadian survey data and extrapolations from US sources, 1.2 to 1.4 million Canadians aged 12 years and above or 4.9% to 5.8% have diabetes, including undiagnosed cases[9]. Among Aboriginal peoples, age-standardized diabetes prevalence rates triple those in the general population, with about 60,000 individuals with diabetes, including undiagnosed cases. The most recent national survey data showed prevalence estimates of diabetes in Canada among 12 year olds and over being 3.2% (NPHS 1996/97), or about 779,000 Canadians. The Aboriginal Peoples Survey (APS 1991) showed that women represent about two-thirds of the First Nations people with a diagnosis of diabetes[10]. The prevalence of diabetes is also high in many other countries particular in those with significant at-risk populations, for examples peoples of African descent, Hispanics, American Indians, and Alaska natives.

H ealth systems worldwide already face rising health care costs, and the challenge of meeting increased demands for health care and prevention within restricted budgets. About 35% of Americans that have diabetes are undiagnosed, 1 million new cases of diabetes diagnosed in adults each year, its annual costs, US$92 billion for direct costs. Of these direct costs, diabetes care accounts for US$23 billion, chronic complications, US$25 billion, and $44 billion for excess prevalence of general medical conditions. The US spends US$40 billion on indirect costs of diabetes, for examples, cost of disability, work loss, and premature death. Besides these costs are the often-devastating effects of its complications on the quality of life of affected persons, and their families. With many of the health problems responsible for the soaring costs of healthcare, including diabetes, preventable, or their consequences controllable, healthcare ICT has a central role to play in managing health costs and optimizing resource utilization. The patient, his or her family, and society all bear the financial burden of diabetes eventually. ICT could help eliminate or reduce the impact of many of this illness' cost drivers. The expected rise in prevalence of diabetes would result in a corresponding increase in its complications, particularly macro- and micro-vascular diseases, but even individuals could take adequate and effective prevention measures to forestall this process using ICT. Pre-diabetic dysglycaemia, or abnormal glucose regulation, characterized by impaired glucose tolerance (IGT) and/or impaired fasting glucose (IFG), has a known association with a high risk of developing type 2 diabetes and cardiovascular disease. Because IGT and IFG emerge well in advance of the diagnosis of type 2 diabetes, the opportunities for primary prevention interventions for type 2 diabetes are not only excellent, but so are those for minimizing its future health and financial burdens. A 2002 DiabCost Australia study using the EQ-5D utility instrument, a validated tool commonly used globally and suited for chronic disease states, found that total (direct plus indirect) health costs of diabetes averaged AU$5360 per year. Furthermore, each person with diabetes received an average AU$5540 in government subsidies such as pensions and sickness benefits. The study also found a significant association between the use of health services and costs linked to diabetes with the presence, and extent of its complications, the cost for individuals with both micro- and macro-vascular complications being 2.4 times more than in people without complicationss. One option for reducing these burdens is pharmacological intervention, and trials such as the Diabetes Prevention Program (DPP) with metformin, and the STOP-NIDDM study with acarbose, have produced significant decreases in the risk of progression to type 2 diabetes in populations with IGT, and suggested positive effects on its cardiovascular sequelae. However, rigorous lifestyle interventions are also effective in preventing or stalling diabetes and healthcare ICT could help in initiating and sustaining such interventions, less intrusively, and more conveniently, affordably, and cost-effectively, for the individual. To start with, individuals could obtain the latest, accurate, and reliable information about diabetes or any health condition of interest from trusted Internet sources, in the comfort of their homes, a major advantage for persons with limited mobility or that live too far away from a healthcare facility. As noted earlier, advances in Internet technologies would make more sophisticated interactive knowledge searches possible, enriching the experience and facilitating the transformation of the knowledge so acquired into health-improving actions. Healthcare providers would likely increasingly embrace the New Jersey model mentioned earlier, and even build on it. In collaboration with enterprising software firms, healthcare providers, in the near future would likely run cutting edge interactive, multimedia, Web Health Programs that would incorporate a variety of services including user-friendly, RSS (Really Simple Syndication)-enabled knowledge base, and interactive, face-to-face encounters with the doctor's secretary, for examples, to schedule or cancel appointments, billing staff, the pharmacist, and, the doctor. It would be possible for individuals to know all that needs knowing about diabetes or any other health condition, including what to do to prevent the occurrence of the disease, or minimize its risks of ever occurring. Besides providing veritable information portals, including information on lifestyle changes that could help reduce the chances of an individual, developing diabetes, for examples, dietary control, and exercises, healthcare ICT could provide other primary prevention opportunities regarding diabetes. It could, for example, by providing information on normal and abnormal levels, help with tracking one's blood sugar levels, for which there currently potable battery-operated, glucometers, requiring just a pin-prick with a built-in lancet. However, we would likely see more user-friendly methods, for example the cell phone technology mentioned earlier, emerge in the near future for such purposes. Measuring the blood sugar levels periodically, particularly by at-risk individuals, would reduce the chances of type 2 diabetes being latent for many years before being diagnosed, as is often the case, by which time, it has started to damage an individual's organs, with consequent morbidity and perhaps mortality that the use of healthcare ICT could help prevent. Given the extent of the potential market for innovative, user-friendly, screening devices for diabetes, does it not make business sense for a software firm to invest in developing technologies that address these problems?

The problems associated with the secondary prevention of diabetes are its early and prompt recognition and treatment to control the disease and prevent complications from developing or slow their progression if already present. Again, what technology should be doing is addressing these problems and issues. Regular blood sugar testing as noted earlier would reveal its dysregulation if any, in individuals with a potential for developing type 2 diabetes. Indeed, it is possible to know quite early if one were pre-diabetic or has developed the disease, and what measures to take in either case using healthcare ICT devices that could measure blood sugar levels regularly. In some cases, diet and exercise would suffice in controlling blood sugar, whereas in others, the individual may need medications. In either case, the results obtained using healthcare ICT device should prompt a visit to one's family doctor, who would advice on the best approaches to treatment. However, such preliminary visits may no longer necessarily be in person, as virtual consultation continues to evolve. Healthcare ICT would also help with the lifestyle changes that the doctor might recommend as either the sole or adjunctive treatment of the condition. Again, exercise routines are likely to be increasingly customized and interactive, with individuals able to videoconference with their physiotherapist and to perform their routines right at home, with the therapist monitoring the type and intensity of the exercises, cardiopulmonary and other vital health data transmitted in real time to the therapist, facilitating the modulation of the entire event. Similarly, individuals would be able to obtain real-time dietary advice, perhaps, even instructions on preparing particularly dietary regimes, whose effects, for example, due to variations in glycemic indices of component food items, the dietician, or doctor, could receive in real-time, via blood sugar measurements. This could facilitate the determination of the most appropriate dietary regimes for the individual, particularly in relation to the anti-diabetic medications on which he or she is, and the necessary adjustments to their dosages. ICT could also help with monitoring, treating, and controlling the complications of diabetes, for examples, its cardiovascular complications.

The tertiary prevention interventions in diabetes should help reduce the occurrence and severity of the long-term disabilities that the disease could cause if not managed properly and even aggressively. Assistive technologies and devices exist that empower such an individual, and indeed those with physical disabilities due to other chronic diseases to live independently, productively, and have a reasonable quality of life despite their disabilities. Visual impairment for example due to diabetic retinopathy, which affects tiny blood vessels in the retina predisposing them to breakdowns, leakages, and blockages, is one of the commonest long-term complications of diabetes, fairly common also, cataracts, and glaucoma. Diabetic retinopathy affects more than 5.3 million Americans aged 18 and older. Estimates vary, but most indicate that there are about 10 million blind and visually impaired people in the United States. Over 1 million Americans more than 40 years old are blind and a further 2.4 million, visually impaired, and 1.3 million legally blind, with central visual acuity of 20/200 or less in the better eye with the best possible correction, as measured on a Snellen vision chart, or a visual field of 20 degrees or less. Estimates show that twice more Americans are at risk for age-related eye diseases in the next three decades, according to the Vision Problems in the U.S. report released March 20, 2002 by the National Eye Institute, in partnership with Prevent Blindness America[11]. About 1.6 million Americans have diabetes complicated with visual impairment or blindness[12]. According to the US Centers for Disease Control and Prevention (CDC), diabetic retinopathy causes between 12,000 and 24,000 new cases of blindness each year. With the population in Canada also ageing, the picture is hardly different. According to Statistics Canada, seniors will constitute about 21% of the population in the year 2026. The Hals Post Census survey (1994) predicted that by the age of 65, one in nine Canadians would experience severe vision loss, and one in four by the age of 85. In 2002, there were 105,000 Canadians registered with Canadian National Institute for the Blind (CNIB) as blind or severely visually impaired, the rate estimated to be increasing by 1000 per month, which would result in a doubling of the number of blind and severely visually impaired Canadians in 2012[13]. However, age-related macular degeneration (AMD) is the commonest cause of blindness and vision impairment in Canadians aged 60 and older, almost one million Canadians affected in 2002 and as Canadians age, the growth rate 77,000 per annum, although diabetic retinopathy, cataracts, and glaucoma are also increasingly common.

Visual impairments could make it difficult for someone with diabetes to inject

his or her insulin or monitor blood sugar levels, not mention perform activities of daily living such as cooking, eating, bathing, and getting dressed. Some software and ICT firms may want to focus on developing technologies that would assist individuals with diabetic retinopathy or disabilities due to other diseases. Examples of such other disabilities are the limitation of movement, even paralysis due to stroke and spinal cord injuries, the tremors due to Parkinson's disease, the swollen and painful joints due to rheumatoid arthritis, or the memory impairment due to Alzheimer's disease and other dementias. There are voice-activated devices or talking blood glucose monitors on the market many, able to attach to the bottom of the medication vial, enabling non-sighted vial identification, and able to record a pharmacist's spoken one-minute message, re-playable as often as required, the chances of alteration or accidental erasure, pretty slim, and they are reusable, and mostly affordable. There are also blood glucose monitoring devices without voice enunciation, and a number of companies manufacture insulin syringe magnifiers, and insulin injection systems or "insulin pens", insulin pumps and other assistive devices for visually impaired diabetes sufferers. Considering the high prevalence of visual impairment due to diabetes, and blindness in general seems likely to be increasingly prevalent in the industrialized world due to changing demographic characteristics, including immigration and ageing, respectively, there is a potentially huge market for healthcare ICT tertiary intervention products. There is no doubt about the worth of R&D investments in developing products that tackle not only the problems and difficulties individuals with visual impairment face, but also those related to the other complications of diabetes such as lower extremity arterial disease, dental diseases, kidney failure, and proneness to infections. All the prevention intervention approaches require the active involvement of the individual, and this participation, research has shown often pays off. Thus, keeping the blood sugar at near normal values, and the blood pressure and cholesterol levels, research has shown clearly reduces diabetes complications[14, 15]. Further, routine preventive care practices for examples regular foot exams, eye exams, and repeated A1C testing help prevent the progression of diabetes complications[16]. However, even with individuals empowered to participate actively in the management of their health conditions, courtesy of innovative healthcare ICT, there is a need to collaborate and share health information with a variety of healthcare professionals involved in their care[17]. This would require the development of other technologies that could connect the individual to these various professionals, and perhaps other agencies and community resources involved in initiating and coordinating a variety of anti-diabetes programs in his or her locale, for examples, support groups, disease and case management, or redesigning diabetes healthcare processes to improve disease outcomes[18]. There is no doubt that the individual would benefit in the long term from such community-oriented preventive interventions. Some interventions are specific for each of the prevention category, others cut across primary, secondary, and tertiary prevention. Health information dissemination for example in primary prevention could simply lead to increase awareness of the disease, which at-risk individuals including those with impaired glucose tolerance in particular would most benefit from, hence should be keenest to employ healthcare ICT for this purpose. With regard, secondary prevention would be health information that stress the need for and type of treatment for different blood glucose levels and that on the possible consequences of not taking those recommended steps. Information dispelling untruths and myths about various aspects of the disease for example infections and the steps to take when they occur would also qualify as secondary interventions. Whereas, information the individual obtains that helps to increase the rates of eye and foot examinations would be tertiary intervention. Clearly, different information technologies would be appropriate for these different tasks, further creating avenues for software and ICT firms to position themselves in niche markets, an opportunity the smaller firms would likely relish.

There are opportunities for developing technologies for individuals to use in

matters relating to their health in many technological domains, for examples, Artificial Intelligence (AI) and robotics, nano-technology, and in genomics, for examples. There would likely be robots that would provide valuable services to the elderly in nursing homes, for example. Such robots might be able to help with dispensing their medications, serving their meals, even monitoring their vital signs round the clock, for example using Bluetooth technology, and alert healthcare professionals if something went wrong. A life size robot is now on the market that could dance with a human, able to anticipate and compute his or her every move during the dance. Such robots could provide effective psychological therapies, for example, dance therapy, to some depressed individuals in future. There might also be robots capable of chatting with humans to a certain extent recording the person's mood via an in-built algorithm, thereby able to monitor someone's mood, and detect when it crosses a certain threshold, raising the appropriate alarm, which could prevent disastrous consequences, such as suicide, in some cases. The manufacture of health consumer products from atoms an d molecules, made possible by nanotechnology, which embraces many areas of research on incredibly small objects, measured in nanometers, one nanometer (nm) being a billionth of a meter, or a millionth of a millimeter would no doubt happen sometime in the near future. Nanotechnology aims to manipulate atoms individually and place them in a pattern to produce a desired structure, for example, using nanogears, about a nanometer wide, to construct a matter compiler, which would arrange atoms and build a macro-scale structure. Progress in nanotechnology has been relentless since researchers at IBM showed, in 1990, that it was possible to manipulate individual atoms by positioning 35 xenon atoms on the surface of a nickel crystal. Nanomachines, termed assemblers, have since emerged, programmable to manipulate atoms and molecules, and to construct products automatically. Nanomachines would be able to replicate anything eventually, ranging from fabric, to water, even food. Indeed, nanoscaled devices will be much more like nature's nanodevices, for examples proteins and DNA. The impact of nanotechnology on the healthcare industry would be enormous. Engineers would construct sophisticated nanorobots that could navigate the human body, transport molecules, manipulate objects, and communicate with doctors via miniature sensors, motors, manipulators, power generators and quantum computers. It is not far-fetched to conjecture an imminent future of nanorobots and "smart drugs" programmed to diagnose diseases and to attack and reconstruct the molecular structure of cancer cells and viruses, rendering them harmless, leaving healthy cells intact. Soon also, rather than use viruses stripped of their native genes for gene-therapy trials as is current practice, to carry therapeutic DNA into a target cell, starburst dendrimers, a class of synthetic molecules capable of sneaking into diseased cells without triggering an immune reaction as viruses often do would do the job instead. Cancer treatment seems to be the main target of nanomedicine, but nanotechnology would also be valuable in other fields for example in coordinating the activities of osteoblasts and osteoclasts thereby preventing osteoporosis. The future patient would receive nanorobots prescribed as a drink to slow or reverse aging. Nanorobots would also be programmed to perform delicate, nanoscale, surgeries, potentially scar-free, and plastic surgeries that could rearrange atoms to give someone an entirely new look. Artificial red blood cells to provide metabolic support in the event of impaired circulation by improving the levels of available oxygen despite reduced blood are no longer fictitious. Despite its potential value, ethical concerns seem to pose a major threat to progress in nanotechnology. From the potential health risks of carbon in nanotubes and nanoparticles, to the so-called "grey goo", a doomsday scenario termed ecophagy in which some imagine that errant armies of self-replicating nanorobots would wage war on human beings and consume all life on earth while cloning themselves, there have been speculations, some wild, others science-based on the ills of this technology. Advances in stem cell research might someday provide the cures for diabetes, cancer, and other diseases. Many of the treatments nanotechnology and gene therapy would offer individuals would be actively involved in delivering, monitoring, and evaluating. The prevention intervention approach discussed above is applicable to any other disease, and facilitates this interactive process. It is also heuristic, revealing underlying disease processes and their consequences, thereby facilitating requirements analysis and the development of appropriate software and other ICT to address stated issues, improve service delivery processes, and solve identified problems. Diligently applied, this approach would likely improve quality of care, clinical outcomes, and the quality of life of the individuals affected by the particular disease. There is little doubt that we are approaching, and quite rapidly too, the era of client-focused, interactive medicine, driven by the changing dynamics of human intercourse, and sustained by scientific and technological progress.

References

1. Bradford W. Hesse; David E. Nelson; Gary L. Kreps; Robert T. Croyle; Neeraj K. Arora; Barbara K. Rimer; Kasisomayajula Viswanath. Trust and Sources of Health Information: The Impact of the Internet and Its Implications for Health Care Providers: Findings from the First Health Information National Trends Survey. *Arch Intern Med.* 2005; 165: 2618-2624.

2. Application of Computer Technology Internet in Mental Health Care

Available at:
http://www.medicalnewstoday.com/medicalnews.php?newsid=32771

Accessed on: December 21, 2005

3. Richard Hillstad, James Bigelow, Anthony Bower, Federico Girosi, Robin Meili, Richard Scoville, and Roger Taylor Can Electronic Medical Record Systems Transform Health Care? Potential Health Benefits, Savings, and Costs *H ealth Affairs*, Vol. 24, Issue 5, 1103-1117 September/October 2005

4. Robert H. Miller, Christopher West, Tiffany Martin Brown, Ida Sim, and Chris Ganchoff. The Value of Electronic Health Records in Solo or Small Group Practices *Health Affairs*, Vol. 24, Issue 5, 1127-1137 September/October 2005

5. David Gans, John Kralewski, Terry Hammons and Bryan Dowd, Medical Groups' Adoption of Electronic Health Records and Information Systems *Health Affairs,* Vol 24, Issue 5, 1323-1333 September/October 2005

6. Worldwide prevalence of diabetes projected to rise. Diabetes Care 2004; 27:1047-53

7. Available at: http://www.aafp.org/x25234.xml

8. Available at: www.adelaide.edu.au/sapo/binary321/DiabCost.pdf Accessed on December 21, 2005

9. Available at: http://www.phac-aspc.gc.ca/publicat/dic-dac99/

10. Available at: http://www.phac-aspc.gc.ca/publicat/dic-dac2/english/50chap6_e.html Accessed on December 21, 2005

11. Available at: http://www.nei.nih.gov/news/pressreleases/032002.asp Accessed on December 24, 2005

12. Saadine, J. B., Narayam, K. M., Engelgau, M. M., Aubert, R. E., Klein, R., & Beckles, G. I. (1999) Prevalence of self-rated visual impairment among adults with diabetes *American Journal of Public Health,* 89, 12001205

13. Aging Population Means More Canadians Facing Blindness
Available at: http://www.cnib.ca/eng/media-centre/stories/natcol_report.htm Accessed on December 24, 2005

14. U.S. Department of Health and Human Services. *Healthy People 2010.* Washington, DC: U.S. Department of Health and Human Services, 2000.

15. UK Prospective Diabetes Study (UKPDS) Group. Tight blood pressure control and risk of macrovascular and microvascular complications in type 2 diabetes: UKPDS 38. *BMJ* 1998; 317 (7160):703-13.

16. American Diabetes Association: Clinical practice recommendations, 2002. *Diabetes Care* 2002; 25 (Suppl 1): S1-147.

17. Committee on Quality Health Care in America, Institute of Medicine.
Crossing the Quality Chasm: A New Health System for the 21st Century. Washington, DC: National Academy Press, 2001.

18. Task Force on Community Preventive Services. Strategies for reducing morbidity and mortality from diabetes through health-care system interventions and diabetes self-management education in community settings. A report on recommendations of the Task Force on Community Preventive Services. *MMWR Recomm Rep* 2001; 50 (RR16):1-15.

Conclusions

H ealth information technologies have become the mainstay of the new health

revolution, the paradigm shift in health toward empowering the consumer, which not only implies more active participation in all matters relating to their health, but also the taking up of increasing responsibility for such matters. In other words, healthcare providers are increasingly obliged to meet the expectations of healthcare consumers, who in turn, should be willing to share in the costs of health services provision. The idea of this consumer-driven healthcare delivery is to create more-discerning healthcare consumers who, presented with the opportunities to choose whom their healthcare providers would be, would demand the best services at affordable prices. This in turn would compel service providers, intent on remaining in business to adopt means that would enhance their competitiveness, including creating novel value propositions for their clients in a bid for competitive edge. One potent approach to acquiring such an edge would be to invest in and implement sophisticated health information technologies, which as we found in the discussions in this book offer immense benefits to health and healthcare. In particular, these technologies enable the provision of targeted patient information. They also facilitate the communication and sharing of patient information among healthcare providers in the same hospital and in different locations, among other benefits, lacking which would be counter-productive to achieving contemporary healthcare delivery goals. For example, such information transmission mentioned above requires the implementation of such technologies such as electronic health records (EHR) systems, which would provide the infrastructure for the achievement of many of the benefits that healthcare ICT offers, for example making available at the point of care (POC) crucial patient information that could help with instituting appropriate treatments, saving lives. Additionally, by reducing morbidities and mortalities in the process, these technologies also help reduce hospitalization rates, medications costs, hence overall healthcare costs, not to mention enhancing patient safety. In countries such as the US, healthcare spending puts arguably the most significant pressure on the economy, which explains, the relentless efforts by governments and the private sector, and indeed other interested stakeholders, toward reducing healthcare costs. The government for example, is investing substantially on healthcare ICT, which it believes, and justifiably so, would help largely in achieving this goal, without compromising health care services. Despite these efforts, the adoption of health information technologies in the health services is not in tandem with the urgent need to deploy these technologies considering the soaring healthcare costs and widespread dissatisfaction with the current state of health services in the country. There are a number of possible reasons for this state of affairs, hence the need to intensify efforts to explore and eliminate whatever the barriers are, which would require increased intersectoral collaboration by all healthcare stakeholders. Different health jurisdictions need to collaborate and of learn from one another's experiences implementing health information technologies. They might just discover something they were doing wrong or a better way to do something similar. For example, a recent report in the *British Medical Journal* examined Kaiser Permanente Hawaii's EHR adoption process, via a survey of health-plan staff members. The study titled "Kaiser Permanente's Experience of Implementing an Electronic Medical Record: A Qualitative Study" noted important junctures in the adoption process, assessed its effect on organizational culture and leadership, and explored an EHR deployment's effects on clinical practice and patient care. The firm stopped deploying the system studied, developed in 2001, for a competing system in 2003, just prior to the commencement of the study. Many of those surveyed for the report reported frustration from the beginning of the implementation, many others, displeasure with the choice of system and a lack of buy-in from clinicians. Others found the EHR system reduced clinical productivity, which affected patient care. The findings prompted the researchers to suggest a participatory process for staff input. The physicians felt that "they were becoming expensive order entry clerks". Thus, there needs to be a clear avoidance of role diffusion in implementing EHR. Would another healthcare organization planning to implement EHR not find the

197

report of this study instructive? Costs are significant barriers to implementing health information technologies. It would be necessary for government to continue to invest in healthcare ICT, and to encourage small medical practices and those in rural areas to do the same. The current efforts to provide healthcare providers with incentives to implement healthcare ICT are commendable, but no doubt, more needs done if we were to achieve the noble objectives of improving healthcare delivery to all.

However, infusing funds into the healthcare ICT diffusion efforts is no panacea to the slow adoption of EHR and other health information technologies. There is also a need for attitudinal change of the end-users of these technologies, particularly healthcare professionals, and the public. This change in attitude requires continuing efforts to make these end-users know the value to healthcare delivery of health information technologies. There would also be a need to reassure them that it is safe and secure to share patient information, the public wary of the privacy and confidentiality of personal health records, healthcare professionals, of ethical violations and of litigation. President Bush did in fact attempt to address such issues in his 2006 State of the Union speech by proposing a cap on malpractice suits. As for reassuring the public, various governments have passed a number of information privacy and confidentiality legislations, for example aspects of the US health insurance portability and accountability Act (HIPAA). They have also passed laws on patient safety, another important concern holding up the widespread adoption of health information technologies, for example the US Patient Safety and Quality Improvement Act of 2005 (S. 720 and HR 663), of July 2005. The Act mandates the Department of Health and Human Services to establish a process for voluntary and confidential medical errors reporting. As experience thus far shows, it is not going to be an easy task promoting the use of health information technologies. However, it is a task worth every ounce of effort put into it. Regional Health Information Organizations are waxing stronger in the US, for example, US National Coordinator for Health Information Technology (ONC) Dr. David Brailer noting recently in his keynote address at the 2006 Annual HIMSS Conference and Exhibition that his office will be focusing its efforts on forming guidelines and minimum standards to help them form and grow. RHIOs will no doubt coalesce into a national health information network (NHIN) in the country, and as Dr Brailer also noted, RHIOs are "crucial" to the move by the US toward an electronic health information system. Yet, it is no news that developing a viable data exchange model for the U.S., on which any NHIN would depend, is going to be anything but easy. Indeed, discussions are ongoing between ONC interoperability standards officials and the four companies HHS chose to create prototypes for a NHIN, namely, Accenture, Computer Sciences Corporation, IBM and Northrop Grumman . According to Dr. John Loonsk, director of interoperability standards for the ONC, most of the prototypes are still to achieve significant information exchange although efforts at improving data exchange seem promising, and the prototypes, still in the first phase of development, and the groups, all face "regional risk factors" solutions to which require strategic approaches. Healthcare ICT confront problems in other countries as well, so much so, in Australia, for example, health ICT experts are calling on Prime Minister John Howard to take control of the wavering national e-health reform agenda. The call is due to increasing dissatisfaction over modifications to plans for the centerpiece HealthConnect network, a feeling that the country's Federal government is trying to heave responsibility for health ICT to the states, and anger over the vision of HealthConnect as a "health market change management strategy," rather than a pillar of the country's enduring shared e-health record. On a more technical plane, some vendors are pushing for the adoption of their version of "portals," to RHIOs arguing that the portal is more important at this point than the EMR, and that doctors need to have access to hospital, radiology and other reports that other providers generate. They hold that a portal could either facilitate this by push or pull technology or "spider" algorithms, presumably, while we wait for EHR/EMR implementations. On a political level, and in a tie vote on February 21, 2006, the Wyoming Senate blocked legislation that would have made the state the first in US to create an EHRnetwork, with some of the Bill's opponents questioning whether the multimillion-dollar system would ever work, others citing privacy concerns. Protestations by proponents that the proposed EHR network would reduce healthcare costs and improve care did not apparently impress the opposing camp. These examples illustrate the difficulties implementing health information technologies face, which hinder progress, and would likely continue to, regarding deploying these valuable technologies. However, our discussions in this book clearly show that there is no going back on the current paths that healthcare trod. The point is for believers in the enormous opportunities that healthcare ICT offers us in improving healthcare delivery to recognize the need for perseverance in their efforts to see the widespread adoption of these technologies in our health systems come to fruition. There is in fact evidence all around that these efforts would yield the desired results, eventually. For example, the American Medical Association, albeit with some members dissenting, recently signed a pact with Congress undertaking to develop over 100 standard performance measures, which doctors will report to the federal government in an effort to improve the quality of care. The deal coincides with efforts of the Bush administration to push "pay for performance" arrangements with a range of healthcare providers in a bid to publicize their performance and couple Medicare payment to quality. Such coupling is also gaining currency in the private sector, where healthcare payers, for examples, consumer groups, insurance companies, and large employers are demanding more information on the quality of care. Does this not tie neatly with the idea of the new healthcare paradigm being the way forward? Does it also not suggest that the implementation of health information technologies by healthcare providers and other industry stakeholders is not negotiable in a consumer-driven healthcare delivery model? It is in fact difficult to conceive of anyone not answering these questions in the affirmative.

www.ingramcontent.com/pod-product-compliance
Lightning Source LLC
Chambersburg PA
CBHW031239050326
40690CB00007B/865